BORDERLINE PERSONALITY DISORDER

INTRODUCING ST -- NEW BPD THERAPY

By DR. PAUL DAWSON

Copyright (c) 2013 by Dr. Paul Dawson

All rights reserved. No part of this book may be reproduced in whole or in part without written permission from the publisher and author, except by reviewers who may quote brief excerpts in connection with a review in a newspaper, magazine, or electronic publication; nor may any part of this book be reproduced, stored in a retrieval system, or transmitted in any form or by any means electronic, mechanical, photocopying, recording, or other, without written permission from the publisher and author.

Printed in the United States of America

Distributed by Create Space & Amazon.Com

TABLE OF CONTENTS:

CHAPTER 1:   MARILYN MONROE & BPD

CHAPTER 2:   "PLAY MISTY FOR ME" & BPD

CHAPTER 3:   "BLIND DATE" & BPD

CHAPTER 4:   "FATAL ATTRACTION" & BPD

CHAPTER 5:   "GIRL, INTERRUPTED" & BPD

CHAPTER 6:   "GIRL, INTERRUPTED" THEMES

CHAPTER 7:   "GIRL, INTERRUPTED" SIGNIFICANCE

CHAPTER 8:   "SINGLE WHITE FEMALE" & BPD

CHAPTER 9:   "THE ROOMMATE" & BPD

CHAPTER 10: "THE CRUSH" & BPD

CHAPTER 11: "MAD LOVE" & BPD

CHAPTER 12: "THE CABLE GUY" & BPD

CHAPTER 13: "NOTES ON A SCANDAL," "INTERIORS" & BPD

CHAPTER 14: "THE CATCHER IN THE RYE" & BPD

CHAPTER 15: "TOM CAPANO, DEADLY SEDUCER" & BPD

CHAPTER 16: AILEEN WUORNOS, FEMALE SERIAL KILLER & BPD

CHAPTER 17: WHO GETS BPD AND WHY?

CHAPTER 18:   MYTHS ABOUT BPD

CHAPTER 19:   SENSATION SEEKING, IMPULSIVITY & SELF-HARM

CHAPTER 20:   EXPLOSIVE FEELINGS & MOODS

CHAPTER 21:   BPD IDENTITY PROBLEMS

CHAPTER 22:   INTERPERSONAL INSTABILITY & BPD

CHAPTER 23:   EXTREME THINKING & BPD

CHAPTER 24:   DISSOCIATION, PARANOIA & BPD

CHAPTER 25:   ASSESSING, DIAGNOSING BPD

CHAPTER 26:   HOW IS BPD DIFFERENTIATED FROM OTHER DISORDERS?

CHAPTER 27:   INDIVIDUAL & GROUP PSYCHOTHERAPY & BPD

CHAPTER 28:   NEUROLOGICAL INDICATIONS FOR BPD

CHAPTER 29:   MEDICATIONS TO TREAT BPD

CHAPTER 30:   ST -- NEW BPD THERAPY

CHAPTER 31:   INTERSELF TEST & SEVEN-SELVES PROFILE

CHAPTER 1:   MARILYN MONROE & BPD

"Sometimes I've got such lousy taste in men... There were times when I'd... run into one of these Hollywood heels at a party and they'd paw me cheaply in front of everybody as if they were saying, *'Oh, we had her.'* I guess it's the classic situation of an ex-whore, though I was never a whore in that sense."

"I was never kept; I always kept myself. But there was a period when I responded too much to flattery and slept around too much, thinking it would help my career, though I always liked the guy at the time. They were always so full of self-confidence and I had none at all and they made me feel better."

"I sometimes felt I was hooked on sex, the way an alcoholic is on liquor or a junkie on dope. My body turned all these people on, like turning on an electric light, and there was so rarely anything human it."

The above comments were made by Marilyn Monroe in an interview at the time she was filming *The Misfits*. I would argue that Marilyn Monroe fits the diagnostic criteria for Borderline Personality Disorder.

The main feature of borderline personality disorder (BPD) is a pervasive pattern of instability in interpersonal relationships, self-image and emotions. People with borderline personality disorder are usually very impulsive.

"Yes, there was something special about me, and I knew what it was. I was the kind of girl they found dead in a hall bedroom with an empty bottle of sleeping pills in her hand," Marilyn Monroe said in *My Story*, her autobiographical work ghostwritten by Ben Hecht, which was tragically prophetic.

This BPD disorder occurs in most by early adulthood. The unstable pattern of interacting with others has persisted for years and is usually closely related to the person's self-image and early social interactions.

The pattern is present in a variety of settings (e.G., not just at work or home) and often is accompanied by a similar lability (fluctuating back and forth, sometimes in a quick manner) in a person's emotions and feelings.

Relationships and the person's emotion may often be characterized as being shallow. On her relationship with the baseball great Joe DiMaggio, Marilyn said:

"Our marriage was a sort of crazy, difficult friendship with sexual privileges. Later I learned that's what marriages often are."

In 1959 when Marilyn's marriage to playwright Arthur Miller was in swift decline, she remarked:

"I guess I am a fantasy... When I married Arthur Miller, one of the fantasies in my mind was that I could get away from Marilyn Monroe through him."

Marilyn had an identity disturbance, such as a significant and persistent unstable self-image or sense of self. This is a symptom of BPD. Chronic feelings of emptiness is another symptom of borderline personality disorder. For example, Marilyn commented on her self-image:

"I always felt I was a nobody, and the only way for me to be somebody was to be -- well, somebody else."

She could escape herself by playing roles in the movies. Marilyn transformed herself into a sex symbol's persona. Pauline Kael, film critic, described the image Marilyn projected to the public:

"She would bat her Bambi eyelashes, lick her messy suggestive open mouth, wiggle that pert and tempting bottom and use her hushed voice to caress us with dizzying innuendoes. Her extravagantly ripe body bulging and spilling out of her clothes, she threw herself at us with the off-color innocence of a baby whore."

George Masters, hairstylist to the stars, observed:

"As a general rule Marilyn would begin turning on about eight hours after I had started with her, while I was applying her lipstick or adjusting her dress. Until then she was a girl you wouldn't look at twice. When she became secure enough to turn into this other person named Marilyn Monroe, then all of a sudden something happened. That's when it was goose bump-time..."

"You could really see it with your own eyes, you could feel it in the room -- the complete transformation, like Dr. Jekyll and Mr. Hyde. Her mannerisms, her gestures, everything was changed, not only her dress and makeup. She was a totally different person, an exploding image, a projection of sexuality and magnetism beyond belief. Even remembering it now I get goose bumps. She was phenomenal to watch."

Transient, stress-related paranoid thoughts or severe dissociative symptoms is another symptom of BPD. Ben Hecht, Marilyn's autobiography ghostwriter had this insight about her:

"The truth about Marilyn Monroe is that she was saved by Hollywood. Fame saved her. The spotlight beating on her twenty-four hours a day made the world seem livable to her... It was the only world in which she could thrive. The real world held only hobgoblins for her, terrors that harried her nights."

The BPD symptom of identity disturbance is further reflected in comments by Catherine David, writer, in her biography, *Simone Signoret*:

"Since the cinema was invented and stars appeared, there was never such a discrepancy between an actress and her image. Marilyn's sensual perfection was all her own invention, a work of art created by herself. But behind the look, beneath the legend, there was nothing but a frightened, abandoned child. She knew that she was only an impostor, and the knowledge hurt her deeply."

Marilyn's pattern of unstable and intense interpersonal relationships characterized by alternating between extremes of idealization and devaluation is a BPD symptom. At times she made frantic efforts to avoid real or imagined abandonment including recurrent suicidal behavior, gestures, or threats which are BPD symptoms. She felt abandoned as a child.

She considered herself a waif -- a woman with a painful past, the parent-less child thrown out of her home, the tortured outcast from society. Marilyn remarked:

"Fame to me certainly is only temporary and a partial happiness -- even for a waif and I was brought up a waif. But fame is not really for a daily diet, that's not what fulfills you. It warms you a bit but the warming is temporary."

Marilyn was born in Los Angeles on June 1st, 1926 -- Norma Jeane Mortensen was her name on her birth certificate. Her mother, Gladys Baker Mortensen turned baby Marilyn over to a foster family on June 13th. Norma Jeane lived in Hawthorne, near L.A., for seven years with the foster parents.

Her mother, Gladys, spent her life from 1934 in mental hospitals. In 1934 Grace McKee, a friend of Gladys, assumed the care and education of Norma Jeane. On June 1st, 1935, Grace was made the court-appointed guardian to Gladys and the legal guardian of Norma Jeane.

In 1938 Norma Jeane was boarded with Ann Lower, an aunt of Grace McKee. Later Marilyn said, "Ana Lower was the first person in the world I ever really loved. She was the only one who loved and understood me."

In 1942, at age 16, Norma Jeane married. Model jobs led to a screen-test at Twentieth Century-Fox in 1947, she signed a standard six-month contract at $75 a week, changed her name to Marilyn Monroe, and her career in movies progressed from then.

In her last completed film, *The Misfits*, Marilyn played the role of Roslyn Taber which reflected her real life -- the waif who was an orphan. The orphan may have a hardened veneer, but it is only a brittle glass facade. Her spirit was buffeted to the breaking point by the blows she has suffered, making her as fragile inside as the innocent is on the outside.

Roslyn Taber in *The Misfits* finds herself without a husband and without resources. But instead of ranting and raving at her fate, she stoically soldiers on. Her docile acceptance of this awful news draws many a savior's eye.

The innocent waif at Marilyn's core led her to always fall for the wrong man. She was like a butterfly trying to escape her suffocating cocoon. But her compliant and obedient nature made it seemingly impossible for her to break free.

As an illustration of Marilyn's pattern of unstable and intense interpersonal relationships -- a BPD symptom -- I am listing some better known lovers she had:

James Dougherty, her first husband, denied that Norma Jeane was raped as a child, claiming that he was Marilyn's first lover and that she was a virgin. They were officially divorced in 1946.

David Conover, an Army photographer, was Marilyn's lover. She asked him, "Do you think I'm made of stone? Don't you find me desirable? We've slept in separate beds for a week!"

Andre de Dienes, photographer, slept with Marilyn. Like Dracula, Andre was from Transylvania.

Joseph M. Schenck, a Twentieth Century-Fox mogul, helped Marilyn's career for sexual favors. He was an older lover who spent time in prison for income tax evasion.

In 1948, Marilyn moved in with this lover -- Fred Karger, Columbia Pictures musical director.

Johnny Hyde, her agent, was another lover who paid to have the lump of cartilage removed from the tip of her nose.

Joe DiMaggio, baseball legend, was Marilyn's second husband.

Hal Schaefer, Twentieth Century-Fox musical director, almost succeeded in killing himself during a secret affair with Marilyn.

Marlon Brando, actor, was a lover Marilyn code named "Carlo".

Arthur Miller, playwright, was her third husband who was accused of being a Communist.

Yves Montand, singer and actor, was Marilyn's lover during the filming of *Let's Make Love*.

Frank Sinatra, singer, actor, friend, lover. Marilyn named her dog in his honor.

Douglas Kirkland, photographer who took shots of her. She seduced him.

Elia Kazan, director, introduced Marilyn to Arthur Miller. Kazan was an unsympathetic character in one of Miller's plays. Kazan said, "Marilyn was a simple, eager young woman, a decent-hearted girl whom Hollywood brought down, legs parted."

Marilyn wrote in a letter: "Kazan said I was the gayest girl he ever knew and believe me, he has known many. But he loved me for one year and once rocked me to sleep one night when I was in great anguish."

Milton Greene, photographer and Marilyn's former business partner and lover.

Charlie Chaplin, Jr., actor, thought it was true love until he caught Marilyn having an affair with his brother.

Milton Berle, comedian, was the master of ceremonies when Marilyn rode a pink elephant at Madison Square Garden. They ended up in bed.

John F. Kennedy, President of the United States, had an affair with Marilyn. One time they were at Bing Crosby's in Palm Springs and Bing offered them a bedroom.

Robert Kennedy, Attorney General of the United States, was Marilyn's lover.

President Sukarno of Indonesia -- reportedly the CIA planned to take blackmail photos of Marilyn in bed with Sukarno.

Robert Slatzer, journalist-filmmaker, claims he and Marilyn were married in Tijuana, Mexico, on October 4, 1952.

Marilyn was interviewed by W.J. Weatherby in a New York City bar and the topic of gay sex came up. She remarked:

"I was remembering Monty Cliff. People who aren't fit to open the door for him sneer at his homosexuality. What do they know about it? Labels -- people love putting labels on each other. Then they feel safe. People tried to make me into a lesbian. I laughed. No sex is wrong if there's love in it."

Marilyn was involved with at least four women in well-known stories. One woman, Natasha Lytess, an acting coach at

Columbia Pictures, was assigned to coach Marilyn who was a starlet in 1948. For the next six years Natasha dedicated herself to Marilyn. Natasha was interviewed for a story and claimed:

"She was mio amore -- my love," Natasha said. "It started when I taught her to kiss. Her sweetness rushed into me. We lived together as man and wife. I was the man... and she was the wife. It was the first affair... of that nature... for me. The only. But there were a lot of women chasing after Marilyn, and after a while, I lost her."

Lili St. Cyr, a striptease queen, a very beautiful blonde, was introduced to Marilyn by Ted Jordan, another lover of Marilyn's. In *Norma Jeane: My Secret Life with Marilyn Monroe*, Ted Jordan, the author, revealed Marilyn was seduced at age six by her foster mother in a relationship that lasted for eight years. Then in her starlet years, Marilyn was involved with an aspiring actress who later became quite famous.

When Marilyn met Lili St. Cyr she said, "To have that kind of presence, to have that kind of sex appeal -- that's the way I have to look."

Soon Lili and Marilyn became friends and she patterned herself after Lili who gave her tips on looking and acting sexier.

"I think Lili's in love with me," Marilyn giggled. "At least she acts that way in bed. She really knows how to please a woman, let me tell you."

After Marilyn was divorced from Joe DiMaggio, on November 5th, 1954, Joe DiMaggio and Frank Sinatra led a crew of men, furnished by Sinatra, and broke down the wrong door in an apartment building at 8122 Waring Avenue in Hollywood.

It was a raid aimed at catching Marilyn in a lesbian relationship. But since the bozos broke down the wrong door they didn't catch her in the act.

Brigitte Bardot, the French star of *And God Created Woman*, met Marilyn at a party for Queen Elizabeth of England in 1956. The two blonde bombshells wound up in the ladies' room together. Bardot adjusted her gown, Marilyn looked at herself in the mirror, smelling of Chanel No. 5. Bardot stood there staring at her.

"She seduced me in thirty seconds," Bardot recounted in her autobiography. A *Globe journalist reported on the "intimate friendship" that developed.*

Bobby Kennedy and Jack Kennedy rejected Marilyn shortly before her death which was apparently a suicide. Some of the conspiracy theories included one that Marilyn had committed suicide as revenge against the Kennedy brothers who used her sexually and discarded her. In *Sudden Endings* by M. J. Meaker, a book that examined famous suicides, Marilyn was quoted:

"I feel a queer satisfaction in punishing people who are wanting me now. But it's not them I'm really punishing. It's the long-ago people who didn't want Norma Jeane."

On the weekend before Marilyn's death, she went with Peter Lawford to the Cal-Neva Lodge at Lake Tahoe to see Frank Sinatra perform. She was rumored to be meeting Joe DiMaggio at Lake Tahoe that weekend.

I have two friends who happened to be at the Cal-Neva Lodge that weekend. One met Frank Sinatra in a Cal-Neva Lodge bar after his show and spoke to him. The other one saw Marilyn that weekend and reported that she was strung-out on drugs and alcohol.

In *Double Cross* by Sam and Chuck Giancana, Sam Giancana claimed to have had sex with Marilyn at the Cal-Neva Lodge that weekend. Sam "Mooney" Giancana, a mob boss from Chicago, said Marilyn was distraught because Bobby Kennedy would not take her phone calls.

Apparently she drank herself into near oblivion and poured out her heart to Mafia boss Sam Giancana over the Kennedy brothers who had dumped her after passionate affairs with them.

In Kitty Kelley's book, *His Way: The Unauthorized Biography of Frank Sinatra*, it was reported that Marilyn tried to commit suicide on that weekend at the Cal-Neva.

But she managed to contact a Cal-Neva operator in time and was rushed to the hospital to have her stomach pumped. Peter Lawford reported that Frank Sinatra was so mad at Marilyn for her suicide attempt that he just snarled at everyone.

Marilyn had a pattern of intense fear of abandonment, a BPD symptom, when she was rejected by lovers.

For borderline personality disorder (BPD) to be diagnosed, at least five of the following signs and symptoms must be present:

1) Intense fear of abandonment (Marilyn was brought up like a waif, an orphan, drifting through life, desperately seeking a home base, being passed from a mentally ill mother to friends, guardians, and foster homes. Her abandonment fears likely originated from her painful childhood.)

2) Pattern of unstable relationships (Marilyn had a well established pattern of many lovers, several failed marriages, and no lasting love relationship right up until her death.)

3) Unstable self-image or sense of identity (Marilyn often stated that she felt like a nobody and escaped herself through movie roles or ran away from Marilyn Monroe's persona by marrying Arthur Miller or Joe DiMaggio.)

4) Impulsive and self-destructive behaviors (She used drugs and alcohol to excess. Marilyn sabotaged her marriages and relationships by frequent secret affairs with other men or women.)

5) Suicidal behavior or self-injury (Marilyn attempted suicide several times and ultimately apparently committed suicide by overdosing on drugs.)

6) Wide mood swings (Despite having great success as a film star, Marilyn bounced from highs to suicidal lows, depressed with her life.)

7) Chronic feelings of emptiness (She complained that she was nothing in reality, that the movie star persona of Marilyn Monroe was just a front. She underestimated herself and her talents.)

8) Anger-related problems, such as frequently losing one's temper or having physical fights (While Marilyn was reported to be angry after being discarded in when love affairs ended, her tendency was to turn anger inward into depression. She was a compulsive potential suicide. Arthur Miller was reported to have saved her three times when she overdosed on pills.)

9) Periods of paranoia and loss of contact with reality... She seems to have been somewhat paranoid and lost contact with reality at times. For example, Marilyn was fired from her last film which she never completed -- Something's Got to Give.

But it was her own fault because she called in sick too many days during shooting. She was mixing sleeping pills, speed pills and alcohol. Marilyn was likely genetically predisposed to the BPD mental disorder because her mother was psychotic and confined to mental institutions.

Marilyn Monroe seems to have had a majority of the BPD signs and symptoms to fit the diagnosis of borderline personality disorder.

CHAPTER 2: "PLAY MISTY FOR ME" & BPD

Play Misty For Me was Clint Eastwood's directorial debut. It is an entertaining thriller about obsession that is a precursor for films like *Fatal Attraction*. Eastwood plays against type as DJ Dave Garver, who works at a jazz station in Carmel, CA. He is usually the strong, silent type who seeks revenge or is an enforcer.

In the film, he is a sensitive ladies man, who reads poetry on the air and plays jazz music. He is also the victim. He has what he thinks is a one-night affair with Evelyn Draper played by Jessica Walter. Evelyn fits the borderline personality disorder diagnosis.

Evelyn claims that there's no strings attached, but that turns out to be the farthest thing from the truth. She stalks Garver, showing up unannounced at his home, at a bar he frequents and in one instance tries to kill herself in his bathroom.

In the meantime, Garver is trying to get back together with his former girlfriend Tobie played by a young Donna Mills. Evelyn trashes Garver's house and almost kills his housekeeper, Birdie (Clarice Taylor) and is taken away by the police and put in an asylum.

Garver thinks it's over, but Evelyn gets out of the mental institution and there is one last chilling scene involving scissors and a knife. Ms. Walter is perfect as Evelyn. She plays the part of a psychotic, unhinged, scornful woman just enough over the top to be scarily believable, but not too over the top to become cartoonish.

Let's take another look at the plot and note the BPD signs and symptoms Evelyn reveals. Dave Garver is a KRML radio jockey who broadcasts nightly from his studio in Carmel-by-the-Sea, California, often incorporating poetry into his program. One night he visits his favorite bar, seemingly by coincidence, meets a woman named Evelyn Draper.

Dave offers to drive Evelyn home and she accepts. Once there, she reveals to him that their meeting was not coincidental. She deliberately sought him out after hearing him mention his favorite bar on his radio show. He guesses that she is a frequent caller who always requests the jazz standard "Misty." Evelyn confirms this an then coerces a clearly uncomfortable Dave into having sex with her.

From that point on, Evelyn prominently displays her borderline personality disorder (BPD). She begins showing up at Dave's house uninvited. She frequently alternates between being in love with him and hating him.

Despite the short duration of their affair, she thinks that he loved her and feels abandoned and lonely. She throws jealous temper tantrums and attempts suicide in his home. Evelyn destroys his carefully constructed career move into management by insulting a woman he meets at a business lunch.

After Dave rejects her one time too many, Evelyn lets herself into his home when he is out. His housekeeper walks in to find her maniacally vandalizing his possessions. Evelyn viciously attacks her with a knife and is subsequently committed to a psychiatric hospital.

For a time, all appears well. Dave has successfully rekindled his relationship with his ex-girlfriend, Tobie Williams, and Evelyn is nowhere to be seen. One night, however, Evelyn calls Dave to tell him that she has been released from the mental hospital and is moving to Hawaii. She quotes Edgar Allen Poe's "Annabel Lee" in reference to her obsessive affection for him.

Later, while Dave is asleep, she unsuccessfully attacks him in his home with a butcher knife and then flees. Dave contacts the police, who begin to search for her.

The next day, Dave warns Tobie to stay away from him until Evelyn is caught. She reluctantly agrees to stay home with her new roommate, a girl named Annabel.

That night, Tobie realizes that Annabel is Evelyn in disguise when she notices the scars from Evelyn's suicide attempt. Evelyn takes Tobie hostage and murders Sgt. McCallum (John Larch), who had come to check on the two women.

Meanwhile at the radio station, Dave makes the connection between Tobie's roommate Annabel and the quote from "Annabel Lee" that Evelyn had earlier recited. Evelyn calls and mockingly tells him that she and Tobie are waiting for him.

He switches from a live show to a tape and rushes to confront her. Arriving at his house, he finds Tobie bound and gagged. Evelyn attacks him again with a butcher knife and he tries to steal the knife away from her.

He eventually punches her in the face, knocking her out a window and down a cliff. Dave and Tobie look down at Evelyn's battered body as Dave's voice on the taped radio show dedicates "Misty" to Evelyn one final time.

Evelyn gets the diagnosis of BPD based on having five or more of the following symptoms:

1) Desperate efforts to avoid real or imaginary abandonment (for example, many stalkers are diagnosed with BPD) -- Evelyn stalks Dave all through the movie story.

2) Intense but unstable relationships, cycling between idealizing and devaluing the other person (Evelyn alternates between being in love with Dave and hating him.).

3) A disturbed self-image or sense of self; many people diagnosed with BPD are chameleon-like, assuming the personality traits they think other people desire them to have (At first Evelyn pretends to be a random woman Dave meets at a bar, then takes her mask off to reveal she's a sort of groupie stalking him.)

4) Impulsive behaviors (for instance, compulsive spending, promiscuous sex, substance abuse, reckless driving, or binge eating). Evelyn pushes Dave into sex in a promiscuous way and continues impulsive stalking.

5) Recurring episodes of suicidal behavior, gestures, or threats or self-injurious behavior. She attempts suicide in his home.

6) Extreme mood swings. Evelyn shifts rapidly between loving and hating Dave. She throws jealous temper tantrums or goes into dark depressions and attempts suicide.

7) Chronic feelings of emptiness. Evelyn immediately feels abandoned, lonely, and empty when Dave rejects her. And this is after one-night of sex with Dave.

8) Inappropriate, extreme anger or difficulty controlling anger. After Dave rejects her, Evelyn vandalizes his possessions at his home like a maniac. She attacks his housekeeper with a knife, then takes Dave's girlfriend, Tobie, hostage, and tries to kill Dave.

9) Episodes of paranoia (the feeling that other people are plotting against you) or dissociation. Dissociation is when one experiences a serious form of emotional numbing, feel detached from your body or yourself, as if your life was happening to someone else. You feel like a shadow of a person rather than a real human being.

Evelyn shows paranoid assaultive tendencies in that she attacks Dave, his housekeeper, and his girlfriend with a butcher knife and scissors.

In summary, Evelyn is a movie character showing aspects of at least the majority of the nine symptoms and signs of BPD.

CHAPTER 3: "BLIND DATE" & BPD

The character David in the comedy movie *Blind Date* demonstrates BPD type behavior. The storyline:

When Walter Davis (Bruce Willis) is set up with gorgeous Nadia Gates (Kim Basinger), the perfect *Blind Date* dissolves into disaster in this sexy comedy caper.

Walter invites beautiful southern belle Nadia to a button-down corporate dinner, expecting to impress his associates with this dazzling beauty. But all hell breaks loose when Nadia has "one too many" and reduces the evening -- and Walter's career -- to shambles. Nadia, after a few alcoholic drinks, flips-out and reveals herself to be a crazy alcoholic.

Bad turns to worse when Nadia's insanely jealous ex-beau David (John Larroquette), discovers them together and decides to annihilate the unsuspecting Walter.

Can true love blossom amidst this hilarious havoc? Will Nadia and Walter ever get down to courting each other instead of courting disaster? Find out in the zany Blind

Date, where first encounters can lead to close encounters of the worst kind.

While David's portrayal of a borderline personality disorder character is rather over-the-top and slapstick, he demonstrates the BPD syndrome. David takes desperate measures to avoid abandonment since Nadia has rejected him. He's her stalker.

David shows unstable relationships with Nadia, his parents, and others in the film. He shows a disturbed self-image with chameleon-like tendencies -- pretending to be a respectable lawyer in court or at his office and then stalking Nadia like a crazed lunatic at other times.

He shows extreme mood swings and inappropriate, extreme anger such as stalking, fighting, and crashing his car. David seems to have revealed most of the BPD symptoms in the movie.

CHAPTER 4: "FATAL ATTRACTION" & BPD

In the thriller film, *Fatal Attraction,* the character Alex Forrest illustrates the borderline personality disorder. Plot:

Dan Gallagher (Michael Douglas) is a successful, happily married New York attorney living in Manhattan when he meets Alexandra "Alex" Forrest (Glenn Close), an editor for a publishing company, through business.

While his wife, Beth (Anne Archer), and daughter, Ellen (Ellen Hamilton Latzen), are out of town for the weekend, he has a passionate affair with Alex. Though he thought it was understood to be a simple fling, she begins clinging to him.

Dan explains that he must go home and Alex cuts her wrists in a suicide attempt. He helps her to bandage them and later leaves. He thinks the affair is forgotten, but she shows up at various places to see him. She waits at his office one day to apologize and invite him to the opera, but he turns her down.

She then continues to telephone until he tells his secretary that he will no longer take her calls. She then phones his home at all hours, and then confronts him saying that she is pregnant and plans to keep the baby.

Although he wants nothing to do with her, she argues that he must take responsibility. She shows up at his apartment (which is for sale) and meets Beth, feigning interest as a buyer. Later that night, he goes to her apartment to confront her about her actions which results in a violent scuffle. In response, she replies that she will not be ignored.

Dan moves his family to Bedford, but this doesn't deter Alex. She has a tape recording delivered to him filled with verbal abuse. She stalks him in a parking garage, pours acid on his vehicle, and follows him home one night to spy on him, Beth, and Ellen from the bushes in their yard. The sight of their family life literally makes her sick to her stomach.

Alex's obsession escalates further. Dan approaches the police to apply for a restraining order against her (claiming that it is "for a client"), to which the lieutenant claims that he cannot violate her rights without probable cause and that the adulterer has to own up to his adultery.

Alex's rage eventually escalates into violence. At one point, while the Gallaghers are not home, Alex kills Ellen's pet rabbit, and puts it on their stove to boil. After this, Dan tells Beth of the affair and Alex's pregnancy. Enraged, she asks him to leave. Before he goes, Dan calls Alex to tell her that Beth knows about the affair. Beth gets on the phone and warns Alex that if she persists, she will kill her.

Without Dan and Beth's knowledge, Alex picks up Ellen at school and takes her to an amusement park, buying her ice cream as well as taking her on a roller coaster. Beth panics when she realizes that she doesn't know where Ellen is.

She drives around searching and rear-ends a car stopped at an intersection and is slightly injured and hospitalized. Alex later drops Ellen off at Gallaghers' house, asking Ellen for a kiss on the cheek.

Dan barges into Alex's apartment and attacks her, choking her and not too short of strangling her. He stops himself, but as he does she lunges at him with a kitchen knife. He overpowers her, but puts the knife down and leaves, with Alex leaning against the kitchen counter, smiling.

He approaches the police about having her arrested, and they start searching for Alex to bring her in for taking

Ellen. Following her release from the hospital, Beth forgives Dan and they return home.

Beth prepares a bath for herself and Alex suddenly appears, again with the kitchen knife. She starts to explain her resentment of her, nervously fidgeting (which causes her to cut her own leg) and then attacks her. Dan hears the screaming and runs in, wrestles Alex into the bathtub and seemingly drowns her.

She suddenly emerges from the water, swinging the knife. Beth, who went searching for Dan's gun, shoots her in the chest, killing her. The final scene shows police cars outside the Gallaghers' house.

As Dan finishes talking with the cops, he walks inside, where Beth is waiting for him. They embrace and proceed upstairs as the camera focuses on a picture of Dan, Beth, and Ellen.

Alex shows most of the criteria for BPD including the typical characteristics of those with borderline personality disorder such as:

A) Disturbance in self concept -- highly variable self-image. When Dan first meets Alex, she comes across as this sophisticated, professional publishing editor.

They have an affair on one weekend, Dan rejects Alex telling her he is happily married, and Alex stresses-out over this by interpreting the rejection very negatively and personally. With intense anger she snaps that he's had his fun and now wants to discard her.

B) Unstable interpersonal relationships -- Alex has a life-or-death need for controlling her romantic relationships.

She stalks, attacks, and tries to kill Dan and his wife in the process of getting revenge.

Alex over-idealizes or devalues Dan depending on her mood. She tries to manipulate Dan into a love relationship by showing up at his apartment, meeting his wife, and calling Dan at all hours at home.

C) Cognitive disturbances -- Alex turns paranoid, plotted against, persecuted when Dan rejects her and moves out of town with his family.

D) Impulsive behaviors -- Alex got into the mess with Dan by impulsively seducing him into a weekend of sex knowing that he was married. Her sexual promiscuity set herself up for a lot of pain which was deepened by her BPD.

E) Labile affect -- She shows sudden, frequent, and intense changes in affect. When Dan attempts to leave her on that first weekend, she at first angrily verbally abuses him. She growls that his excuse to go home is pathetic.

Alex says she'd have more respect for him if he just told her to "fuck off." Her anger, emptiness, loneliness, or abandonment feelings are expressed as rage or bitterness and despondency. She then cuts her wrists in a suicide gesture to manipulate Dan into staying with her.

F) Functional failures -- Alex is a newly hired editor at the publishing house and by her BPD behavior it is implied that her emotional instability and cognitive disturbances prevent her from reaching her potential in her professional field of choice. But because of her BPD she is unable to successfully apply her abilities.

G) Self-destructive activity -- Alex's self-destructive behavior such as attempting suicide and stalking overlaps with her impulsive behavior. She kidnaps Dan's daughter, kills her pet rabbit, pours acid on his car, leaves an abusive and profane tape recording for him, and stalks Dan.

In summary, the Alex character portrays most of the BPD symptoms to fit the BPD diagnosis requiring five or more of the nine symptoms and signs of BPD:

1) Desperate efforts to avoid real or imaginary abandonment as shown by Alex stalking Dan, getting violent with him and his wife, kidnapping his dauplter, etc.

2) Intense but unstable relationships -- she seduced Dan into a one-weekend sex affair, cycles between idealizing and devaluing Dan, and proceeds to antagonize Dan and his wife.

3) A disturbed self-image or sense of self -- Alex is chameleon-like in initially charming and seducing Dan, presenting herself as a single, professional woman with sex appeal.

Then she takes off her mask and stalks him, escalates her crimes against him and his family into kidnapping and attempted murder.

4) Impulsive behaviors -- Alex's promiscuous sexual behavior -- she seduces Dan after having a drink with him despite not knowing him -- leads to a self-destructive outcome.

5) Recurring episodes of suicidal behavior, gestures, threats or self-injurious behavior. Alex cuts her wrists in a suicide attempt to manipulate Dan into staying with her.

6) Extreme mood swings -- she is very happy and high one moment with Dan on that first weekend of their affair. Then she's depressed, in a rage or suicidal when Dan starts to leave or later rejects her.

7) Chronic feelings of emptiness -- Alex sits in her apartment depressed, turning the lamp on and off, after Dan rejects her invitation to the opera.

8) Inappropriate, extreme anger or difficulty controlling anger. She's infuriated when Dan tries to go home that first weekend. Then she cycles through all kinds of negative feelings as she stalks him throughout the film.

9) Episodes of paranoia -- the feeling that other people are plotting against you or dissociation. Dissociation is an abnormal psychological state in which one's perception of oneself and/or one's environment is altered significantly.

Alex is somewhat paranoid as shown by her reaction to Dan rejecting her. She overreacts to a logical reality -- she knew Dan was married to begin with. So why is she suicidal, depressed, in a rage, stalking him, and ultimately trying to kill him and his wife?

CHAPTER 5: "GIRL, INTERRUPTED" & BPD

"Girl, Interrupted" -- the movie:

Winona Ryder and Angelina Jolie starred in the film version of Susanna Kaysen's memoir "Girl, Interrupted". Ryder played the Kaysen character.

Mark Deming wrote a synopsis of the movie "Girl, Interrupted":

In 1967, 19-year-old Susanna (Winona Ryder) feels that "reality is becoming too dense" and is diagnosed with Borderline Personality Disorder. The doctor suggests to her parents that she be committed to the Claymore Hospital, and she spends the next 18 months struggling with her troubled psyche and the bizarre world of the institution.

Susanna bonds with several other patients, including Lisa (Angelina Jolie), Polly (Elizabeth Moss), and Georgina (Clea DuVall). As she realizes that Lisa is potentially dangerous and truly needs help, Susanna begins to work harder with her psychiatrist (Vanessa Redgrave) and the nurse on the ward (Whoppi Goldberg).

But Susanna soon learns that getting out of the hospital is not as easy as getting in. Girl, Interrupted was based on the autobiography of Susanna Kaysen, who really did spend a year-and-a-half in the McLean Psychiatric Hospital in Belmont, Massachusetts.

Peter Stack wrote a movie review of "Girl, Interrupted":

Sappy 'Girl' Lacks Character Development -- "Girl, Interrupted" delivers an assured, finely tuned performance by Winona Ryder. In fact, it's got what it takes to be called a great Winona Ryder movie.

But overall, this look at a confused teenager's experiences in a mental hospital is a sappy, muddled production that misses the jarring tone of the autobiographical book by Susanna Kaysen on which it is based. That's not to say the film fails to entertain. It's just that there is not much power.

Ryder's sensitive performance almost saves the film, but it also works against the whole. For all her intensity and brave acting, her portrayal of a troubled young woman results in a character who's hard to care about.

It's not really her fault -- fact is, budding writer Susanna (Ryder) is never in any kind of dramatic jeopardy. She's mixed up for a while, and then she's not mixed up. Mostly she's a witness to the dire straits of other characters.

But Ryder is terrific as a confused middle-class waif who's been hit on by a family friend twice her age and who sees a messed-up '60s world. Her uptight parents and a psychiatrist collude to persuade Susanna to check herself into a swanky private mental hospital in 1967 shortly after graduating from high school.

In the cold confines of Claymore -- it looks more like a New England college campus than a mental hospital -- Susanna develops unexpected friendships with sister "inmates."

Georgina (Clea DuVall) is obsessed with the "Wizard of Oz." Daisy (Brittany Murphy) is a spoiled brat with a dark history. Janet (Angela Bettis) is hazy and out of touch, and Polly (Elisabeth Moss) is a burn victim scarred inside and out.

Susanna also meets Lisa (Angelina Jolie), an acerbic rebel who keeps escaping and being returned by authorities for more extreme sedation and shock treatments. She's a shocking girl, too -- a foul-mouthed, bullying, brazen seductress.

The young women have a kindly warder in a nurse named Valerie (Whoppi Goldberg). But the hospital is overseen by a cool, imperious psychiatrist, Dr. Wick (Vanessa Redgrave). Handsome outsider Toby (Jared Leto) wants Susanna to run away with him (why she doesn't is the movie's oddest twist).

Susanna's intense eyes, her wincing glances and brooding expression reveal the roil of emotions eating at her. Viewers will admire the actorly qualities Ryder brings to the part, and the fine photography of changing seasons by cinematographer Jack Green.

But "Girl, Interrupted" never catches fire. A too-tidy, calculated effort to steer the story toward a melodrama of sisterhood, with comic asides, keeps it light and sappy and mostly unsatisfying. It's no *Snake Pit*, no *One Flew Over the Cuckoo's* Nest.

Perhaps the film's biggest muddle is that Susanna is the character viewers may care about least. The film's other characters are more interesting, more bruised, more haunting, yet they're barely fleshed out.

Lisa, for example, is the most vital and fascinating, even though Jolie pushes her to more caricature than character. She's strident, angry, smart, sexy and challenging. But we get little more than her brash surfaces and outbursts. She's girl, in your face. The whys and wherefores are hardly explored.

"Girl, Interrupted" -- the novel:

Kaysen's novel, based on her personal experience, encompasses horror and razor-edged perception while providing vivid portraits of her fellow patients and their keepers in McLean Hospital, in Belmont, Massachusetts, which is a mental institution.

It is a brilliant evocation of a "parallel universe" set within the kaleidoscopically shifting landscape of the late sixties. "Girl, Interrupted" is a clear-sighted, unflinching document that gives lasting and specific dimension to our definitions of sane and insane, mental illness and recovery.

The plot of "Girl, Interrupted" does not follow a linear storyline, but instead the author provides personal stories through a series of short descriptions of events and personal reflections on why she was placed in the psychiatric hospital.

She begins by talking about the concept of a parallel universe and how easy it is to slip into one, comparing insanity to an alternate world. She discusses how some people fall into insanity gradually and others just snap.

Kaysen also details the doctor's visit before first going to the hospital and the taxi ride there at the beginning of the book before launching into the chronicles of her time at the hospital.

"Girl, Interrupted" -- Plot Summary:

In April 1967, 18-year-old Susanna Kaysen is admitted to McLean Hospital after attempting suicide by overdosing on pills. She denies that it was a suicide attempt to a psychiatrist, who suggests she take time to regroup in McLean, a private mental hospital.

Borderline Personality Disorder: Susanna is diagnosed with borderline personality disorder (BPD), and her stay extends to 18 months rather than the proposed couple of weeks.

Fellow patients Polly, Cynthia, Lisa, Lisa Cody, Georgina and Daisy contribute to Susanna's experiences at McLean as she describes their personal issues and how they come to cope with the time they must spend in the hospital. Susanna also introduces the reader to particular staff members, including Valerie, Dr. Wick and Mrs. McWeeney.

Susanna reflects on the nature of her illness, including difficulty making sense of visual patterns, and suggests that sanity is a falsehood constructed to help the "healthy" feel "normal" in comparison. She also questions how doctors treat mental illness, and whether they are treating the brain or the mind.

During her stay, Susanna undergoes a period of depersonalization, where she bites open the flesh on her hand after she becomes terrified that she has "lost her bones."

Depersonalization is a sense that one has lost contact with one's own personal reality (e.G., "My body feels strange, like it's not my own.").

She develops a frantic obsession with the verification of this proposed reality and even insists to see an X-ray of herself to make sure. This hectic moment is described with shorter, choppy sentences that show Kaysen's state of mind and thought processes as she went through them.

Also, during a trip to the dentist with Valerie, Susanna becomes frantic after she wakes from the general anesthesia, when no one will tell her how long she was unconscious, and she fears that she has lost time. Like the incident with her bones, Kaysen here also rapidly spirals into a panicky and obsessive state that is only ultimately calmed with medication.

After leaving McLean, Susanna mentions that she kept in touch with Georgina and saw Lisa, who was about to board the subway with her son and seemed, although quirky, to be sane.

Characters in "Girl, Interrupted":

There are two main groups of characters, the patients and the staff. In addition to those there are her parents, her boyfriend and various other minor characters such as her former boss.

The Patients:

Susanna Kaysen -- The autobiographical main character, Susanna Kaysen is admitted to a psychiatric ward to be treated for borderline personality disorder (BPD) following a suicide attempt.

She voluntarily admits herself after a short consultation with a psychiatrist who is also an acquaintance of the family. She is told that she will only be staying there for a few weeks, but it turns out to be close to two years instead.

Throughout the book, she frequently contrasts the time of the consultation, twenty minutes, to the time she ended up spending there.

Lisa Rowe -- Lisa is diagnosed as a sociopath, but whether she actually is one is left open to interpretation.

The term "sociopath" is generally known as antisocial personality disorder (APD) in the Diagnostic and Statistical Manual (DSM).

In a nutshell, people with antisocial personality disorder have little regard for other people, their rights, or their feelings. Many of them blatantly break society's rules and frequently end up in jail. Some of them act with extreme violence with no remorse for their actions or compassion for their victims.

On the other hand, some people with APD aren't particularly aggressive, but they may derive a sadistic sense of pleasure from conning other people. Paradoxically, they often exude charm and charisma.

APD afflicts about 2 percent of the general population, with men significantly outnumbering women. However, in prisons, 50 to 80 percent of the inmates have this disorder.

Typical symptoms of APD: irresponsible, deceitful, dishonest, impulsive, aggressive, irritable, indifferent, guiltless.

Lisa periodically escapes from the hospital, only to be found a day or two later and re-admitted. She is usually happy enough to be back though she does put up a fight when restrained.

She is an ex-junkie who never sleeps and barely eats, and enjoys making trouble for the staff. She apparently takes some pride in her diagnosis. Although she has a therapist assigned to her, she never actually sees him. Lisa is not in contact with her family except her brother, but the extent of their contact is not described.

Lisa also has a lawyer, though it appears he is mostly used to threaten the staff if she doesn't get what she wants. Her behavior is wildly unpredictable, and while she can be kind, she is also capable of cruelty towards the other patients. For example, Lisa has an ongoing rivalry with Lisa Cody that ends in Lisa Cody reverting to drugs.

Polly Clark -- She is a disfigured patient hospitalized for schizophrenia and depression.

"Schizophrenia" is considered a more serious condition that frequently involves delusions, severely disordered thinking, and/or hallucinations.

Polly has severe scarring on her body, the result of setting herself on fire. According to Kaysen, because of the sheer guts it took to actually do it, Polly is highly respected for her courage, to the extent that none of the patients will ask why she did it.

During Polly's first year at the hospital, she appears calm and even cheerful: "Life was hellish, she knew that. But, her smile hinted, she'd burned all that out of her."

But one day she suddenly breaks down and begins to scream inconsolably, as if realizing for the first time her appearance and the permanency of it. Kaysen then realizes that while the other patients might be released from the hospital, Polly is trapped forever in her scarred body.

Georgina Tuskin -- Hospitalized because of schizophrenia, Georgina is Susanna's roommate at the institution. The two of them are considered the healthiest patients on the ward and are good friends throughout the novel.

Georgina apparently experienced her first symptoms after an episode in a movie theater where she suddenly felt as if the darkness had surrounded her completely. It is not clear what the immediate reason for her diagnosis is. She also has a boyfriend in the hospital named Wade.

Lisa Cody -- She is admitted while Kaysen is there and from the beginning looks up to Lisa Rowe. She is diagnosed as a sociopath (APD -- antisocial personality disorder) too, though Rowe questions this and is clearly annoyed that she is no longer the only sociopath there.

A former drug addict like Rowe, she tries hard to defend herself from Lisa Rowe's accusations that she isn't "real". She eventually escapes and is apparently found by Lisa Rowe during one of her escapes from the hospital. Lisa Rowe tells the other girls with pride that Lisa Cody has become a "real" drug addict. Her fate after her escape is not described any further.

Daisy Randone -- A thin girl who is admitted to the hospital seasonally, according to Susanna, coming before Thanksgiving and staying through Christmas every year. She has a single room, where she spends most of her time.

The other girls think she is addicted to laxatives and will only eat chicken, and only in her room. However, after letting Lisa Rowe into her room, Lisa reports back to the rest of them that she only needs the laxatives because of all of the chicken.

She peels off the meat and keeps the carcasses, saying that when she has 14 carcasses, it's time to leave the hospital, possibly due to obsessive compulsive disorder. Daisy's father visits her quite often, and it is implied he has incestuous feelings for her.

Daisy eventually commits suicide on her birthday. Susanna describes her as "sexy" and says Daisy had a spark that the rest of the girls lack. Daisy is reclusive and often refuses to be social.

She hates it when anyone goes near her and is hostile when people approach her. However, she does allow Lisa Rowe to enter her room. Sometimes they even share cigarettes, indicating that Daisy does respect Lisa out of all the other patients on the ward.

Torrey -- An ex-drug addict. She was put into the ward after her parents discovered her promiscuity. She is the best friend of all the fellow patients. Her parents take her out against her will, and take her back to Mexico, where she believes she will become an amphetamine addict again.

She describes Mexico, saying "Being in Mexico means being dead and shooting speed to feel like you're not quite dead." The girls do try to help her with an escape plan. They pool their money for her to help her, but eventually that plan is ruined. Torrey is too afraid to do it. Valerie gives her a cup of thorazine just prior to her departure to calm her down.

Though she only appears for a short time, she is an important character. Kaysen distinguishes between those put there indefinitely by parents willing to pay without questioning the progress of their treatment vs. those whose parents are not willing to do so. Torrey is used as an example of the latter group.

Alice Calais -- At first she seems quiet and, in Kaysen's own words, "Alice is not too crazy." But she eventually breaks down and is taken to maximum security after about a month.

When the girls go to visit her they find that she has painted herself and the walls in her seclusion room with her own feces. Most of the other patients believe she was "raised in a closet" because she is ignorant about the trivial things in life.

For example, she has never tasted honey and doesn't know how it tastes. She is also completely unaware that her last name is a well-known location in France. She is overwhelmed in awe when she hears of the Hundred Years' War. It is not explained what happens to her after the girls visit her.

Wade -- Georgina's boyfriend, also a patient. Wade entertains the female patients with stories about his father, who he claims to be a CIA agent. He is prone to violent outbursts, which eventually results in his being moved to the maximum-security ward.

Cynthia Crowley -- A severely depressive patient, who undergoes weekly electro-convulsive therapy. There are only a few references to her in the novel and she isn't really a major character in it.

The Staff:

Valerie -- The head nurse on the ward. She works there during the day and, though she can be strict, she is generally liked by the patients and Kaysen in particular. She is described as down to earth and rarely uses the psychiatric terms used by the therapists, which is something that Susanna herself despises.

Kaysen recalls her as honest and direct. Kaysen also mentioned that Valerie's hair is very, very long and that the girls all love it. Sometimes, they are able to coax her into taking it out of its stiff braid-bun and show them how she braids it.

Mrs. McWeeney -- The evening nurse on the ward. Described as the exact opposite of Valerie and very much disliked by the patients. Kaysen recalls her as "clearly nuts." Valerie does not like her and tends to ignore her, although she does describe her as a professional when the patients complain to her.

Although the patients don't like her, they recognize that she needs to earn a living and that she has to work somewhere for that to happen.

Dr. Wick -- The consultant psychiatrist. She is described as very old-fashioned and easy to embarrass. Susanna purposely tries to embarrass her, deliberately saying things that she knows Dr. Wick will react to, during their sessions together.

She has previously worked in Africa and her direct contact with the patients is very limited, talking to them for only a matter of minutes in a session.

Melvin -- Kaysen's late therapist and analyst. Susanna says that the two of them used to be good friends and that she once enjoyed sessions with him. According to her, he was old, balding, and slightly unattractive. Susanna would go into his office sometimes and just sit there in silence because there wasn't very much silence in the hospital and she needed a break.

However, this relationship was short-lived. Melvin rolled into the hospital parking lot, and, when greeted enthusiastically by Susanna, refused to entertain her. Her opinion of him spiraled downward from that point.

CHAPTER 6: "GIRL, INTERRUPTED" & BPD

The book explores several themes related to mental illness and society's interpretation of it.

1) Mental illness vs. conformity:

Although Kaysen does admit that she was going through a very difficult time, she questions the validity of her diagnosis and to what degree it could be applied universally to anyone showing nonconformist behavior.

She recalls the other patients' mental conditions and finds it hard to relate them to her own problems. She also describes the stigma that follows from having been hospitalized for mental illness and how she eventually stopped telling people in order to avoid the negative reaction.

2) Hospitalization as treatment:

Kaysen elaborates through parts of the book on her thoughts about how mental illness is treated. She explains that families who are willing to pay the rather high costs of hospitalization do so to prove their own sanity.

Once on member of the family is hospitalized, it becomes easier for the rest of the family to distance themselves from the problem. Then they can create a clear boundary between sane and the insane. Recognizing a family member or friend as insane makes others around them, says Kaysen, compare themselves to that individual.

Hospitalization allows for distance from this questioning of self that makes us so uncomfortable. Her view that mental illness often includes the entire family means the hospitalized family member becomes an excuse for other family members not to look at their own problems. This explains the willingness to pay the high financial costs of hospitalization.

3) Treating the brain vs. the mind:

An important issue in Kaysen's view is the distinction betweeen the treatment of the brain versus the treatment of the mind. She uses an example with two interpreters, one reacting to one's senses and another that processes and evaluates the results from the first interpreter.

She describes mental illness as the failure of the second interpreter to correctly dismiss false interpretations by the first interpreter. She compares this with the chemical reactions of the brain and concludes that those who treat mental illness with drugs are treating the brain whereas therapy is aimed at treating the mind. Though she does not dismiss the use of drugs, she is critical of them.

4) Freedom:

Through parts of the book she describes the trade-off between being a patient in a mental institution and being free in the conventional sense of the word. Though restricted by a complex set of rules she also describes how not being out in the real world sets her free from the expectations of parents and society when it comes to education and work.

Though she describes the hospital as a womb you can't get out of, she also explains the difficulties she had prior to being hospitalized and how the pressure increasingly got to her.

She evaluates the benefits of being in the hospital and being in the outside world -- two parallel universes, as she said in the introduction, that each present one with many freedoms of different kinds.

The hospital provides freedom from responsibility, but is also a prison in that many freedoms and choices that the patients would have outside the hospital are taken away.

5) Freedom vs. captivity:

When Kaysen enters McLean Hospital, she quickly comes to understand that although captivity appears to require the surrender of freedom, the opposite is often true. The ward is organized to keep patients exposed to staff scrutiny at all times. With nurse checks at frequent intervals, every room is essentially public except for one.

The "seclusion room" sits at the farthest reach of the main hallway, intended for out-of-control patients who pose harm to others or simply make too much of a disturbance. Patients can also choose to be placed in the room, prompting Kaysen to remark, "freedom was the price of privacy."

Here, a patient can be blessedly alone for a period, free from scrutiny and company but, like the hospital in comparison to the outside world, confined to even tighter quarters. The seclusion room is a microcosm for the entire experience of confinement to the hospital.

Kaysen notes that McLean is "a refuge as much as a prison." Without school, a job, bills, parents, or the outside world to deal with, the girls are free to ignore responsibility, even as that responsibility has been taken from them. Kaysen finds that this apparent paradox isn't confined to the hospital.

After nearly two years at McLean, Kaysen looks for means to leave but finds that her hospital stay stigmatizes her in the eyes of employers. A marriage proposal turns her circumstances on their head.

"Everyone could understand a marriage proposal," she writes, despite nearly total uncertainty about the appropriateness of her fiancé or the appeal of marriage itself. The engagement frees Kaysen from the confinement of the hospital, but it limits her opportunities.

Kaysen's BPD Diagnosis:

In a chapter entitled "My Diagnosis" Kaysen turns the tables on the shrinks who diagnosed her. She includes copies of her case records and reports stating her intake diagnosis in April of 1967.

Her "established diagnosis, mental disorder" is "Borderline Personality" (BPD). The diagnostic impression at admission is listed as:

1) Psychoneurotic depressive reaction.

2) Personality pattern disturbance, mixed type. R/O Undifferentiated Schizophrenia.

Her A) diagnosis and B) prognosis at discharge 18 months later in 1968 is also included on another page of her case file:

A) Discharge summary -- Formal Diagnosis:

"Schizophrenic reaction, paranoid type (borderline) -- currently in remission. Patient is functioning on a passive-aggressive personality, passive-dependent type."

B) Prognosis:

"The resolution of the depressive affect and suicidal drive should be expected as a result of the hospitalization. The degree of personality integration and ego function which may be achieved for the long term is hard to predict."

"We may say that with a good intensive working relationship in therapy and a successful relationship to the hospital the patient may be able to achieve a more satisfactory means of adapting."

"Nevertheless because of the chronicity of the illness and the basic deficiencies involved in personality structuring, a more complete recovery is not to be expected at this time."

"However, the patient may learn to make more wise choices for herself within the boundaries of her personality so that she is able to achieve a satisfactory dependent relationship if necessary which will sustain her for a long period of time."

Borderline Personality Disorder -- Definition:

Kaysen outlines the features of BPD from the DSM (1987). While she was hospitalized in the late 1960s, *Girl,*

Interrupted was published in 1993. Kaysen defines BPD in 12 points:

1) "An essential feature of this disorder is a pervasive pattern of instability of self-image, interpersonal relationships, and mood, beginning in early adulthood and present in a variety of contexts."

2) "A marked and persistent identity disturbance is almost invariably present. This is often pervasive, and is manifested by uncertainty about several life issues, such as self-image, sexual orientation, long-term goals or career choice, types of friends or lovers to have, and which values to adopt. The person often experiences this instability of self-image as chronic feelings of emptiness and boredom."

3) "Interpersonal relationships are usually unstable and intense, and may be characterized by alternation of the extremes of overidealization and devaluation. These people have difficulty tolerating being alone, and will make frantic efforts to avoid real or imagined abandonment."

4) "Affective instability is common. This may be evidenced by marked mood shifts from baseline mood to depression, irritability, or anxiety, usually lasting a few hours or, only rarely, more than a few days. In addition, these people often have inappropriate intense anger with frequent displays of temper or recurrent physical fights."

"They tend to be impulsive, particularly in activities that are potentially self-damaging, such as shopping sprees, psychoactive substance abuse, reckless driving, casual sex, shoplifting, and binge eating."

5) "Recurrent suicidal threats, gestures, or behavior and other self-mutilating behavior (e.G., wrist-scratching) are common in the more severe forms of the disorder. This

behavior may serve to manipulate others, may be a result of intense anger, or may counteract feelings of 'numbness' and depersonalization that arise during periods of extreme stress..."

6) "Associated Features. Frequently this disorder is accompanied by many features of other Personality Disorders, such as Schizotypal, Histrionic, Narcissistic, and Antisocial Personality Disorders."

"In many cases more than one diagnosis is warranted. Quite often social contrariness and a general pessimistic outlook are observed. Alternation between dependency and self-assertion is common. During periods of extreme stress, transient psychotic symptoms may occur, but they are generally of insufficient severity or duration to warrant an additonal diagnosis."

7) "Impairment. Often there is considerable interference with social or occupational functioning."

8) "Complications. Possible complications include Dysthymia (depressive neurosis), Major Depression, Psychoactive Substance Abuse, and psychotic disorders such as Brief Reactive Psychosis. Premature death may result from suicide."

9) "Sex Ratio. The disorder is more commonly diagnosed in women."

10) "Prevalence. Borderline Personality Disorder is apparently common."

11) "Predisposing and Familial Pattern. No information."

12) "Differential Diagnosis. In Identity Disorder there is a similar clinical picture, but Borderline Personality Disorder preempts the diagnosis of Identity Disorder if the criteria for Borderline Personality Disorder are met, the disturbance is sufficiently pervasive and persistent, and it is unlikely that it will be limited to a developmental stage."

Kaysen's view of her diagnosis:

"I'm tempted to try refuting it, but then I would be open to the further charges of 'defensiveness' and 'resistance,'" Kaysen reasoned. She then breaks up her Borderline Personality Disorder description and comments on each part:

A) Uncertainty about several life issues, such as self-image, sexual orientation, long-term goals or career choice, types of friends or lovers to have...

Kaysen is critical of the BPD diagnostic definition: "I still have that uncertainty. Is this the type of friend or lover I want to have? I ask myself every time I meet someone new..."

She asks, "What does *borderline personality* mean, anyhow? It appears to be a way station between neurosis and psychosis: a fractured but not disassembled psyche. Though to quote my post-Melvin psychiatrist: 'It's what they call people whose lifestyles bother them.'"

Kaysen wonders if BPD is just another passing psychiatric fad or diagnostic flavor-of-the-month -- she quotes an analyst on Freud: "Freud and his circle thought most people were hysterics, then in the fifties it was psychoneurotics, and lately, everyone's a borderline personality... Maybe in another twenty-five years BPD won't be in the DSM (Diagnostic & Statistical Manual)."

B) Instability of self-image, interpersonal relationships, and mood... uncertainty about... long-term goals or career choice.

She brushes this part aside by asking, "Isn't this a good description of adolescence? Moody, fickle, faddish, insecure: in short, impossible."

C) Self-mutilating behavior (e.G., wrist-scratching). This behavior may... counteract feelings of "numbness" and depersonalization that arise during periods of extreme stress.

Kaysen admits she was doing wrist-banging: "Wrist-banging -- slow, steady, mindless... It was cumulative injury, so each bang was tolerable. I spent hours... banging my wrist." She said that she could conceal wrist-banging so she preferred it.

Kaysen said, "I'd had an earlier period of face-scratching. If my finger-nails hadn't been quite short, I couldn't have gotten away with it... But I looked bad enough that people asked, 'Is something wrong with your face?' So I switched to wrist-banging... I was demonstrating, externally and irrefutably, an inward condition."

D) Quite often social contrariness and a general pessimistic outlook are observed.

Kaysen questions, "What do you suppose they mean by 'social contrariness'? Putting my elbows on the table? ...Disappointing my parents hope that I would go to a first-rate university? ...I'll admit to the general pessimistic outlook. Freud had one too."

She points out that her discharge sheet in her case records said she had *recovered*: "Recovered. Had my personality crossed over that border, whatever and wherever it was, to resume life within the confines of the normal? Had I stopped arguing with my personality and learned to straddle the line between sane and insane?"

E) The person often experiences this instability of self-image as chronic feelings of emptiness or boredom.

Kaysen complained that her parents and teachers were trying to push a round peg into a square hole:

"My chronic feelings of emptiness or boredom came from the fact that I was living a life based on my incapacities, which were numerous. A partial list follows. I could not and did not want to: ski, play tennis, or go to gym class, attend to any subject in school other than English and biology, write papers on any assigned topics... plan to go or apply to college, give any reasonable explanation for these refusals."

On her self-image issue:

"My self-image was not unstable. I saw myself, quite correctly, as unfit for the educational and social systems... But my parents and teachers did not share my self-image."

"Their image of me was unstable, since it was out of kilter with reality and based on their needs and wishes... One of my teachers told me I was a nihilist. He meant it as an insult but I took it was a compliment... Boyfriends and literature. How can you make a life out of those two things? ...I did."

Kaysen tackled the issue of emptiness and boredom:

"Emptiness and boredom: what an understatement. What I felt was complete desolation. Desolation, despair, and depression," she complained.

F) This (BPD) disorder is more commonly diagnosed in women.

She attacks this part of the diagnostic description from a sort of feminist viewpoint: "Note the construction of that sentence. They did not write, 'The disorder is more common in women.' It would still be suspect, but they didn't even bother trying to cover their tracks... Many disorders, judging by the hospital population, were more commonly diagnosed in women. Take, for example, 'compulsive promiscuity.'"

Kaysen then compares the treatment of males vs. females:

"How many girls do you think a seventeen-year-old boy would have to screw to earn the label 'compulsively promiscuous'? Three? No, not enough. Six? Doubtful. Ten? ...Probably in the fifteen-to-twenty range, would be my guess -- if they ever put that label on boys, which I don't recall their doing."

G) On the potentially self-damaging activities:

"In the list of six 'potentially self-damaging' activities favored by the borderline personality, three are commonly associated with women (shopping sprees, shoplifting, and eating binges) and one with men (reckless driving). One is not 'gender-specific,' as they say these days (psychoactive substance abuse). And the definition of the other (casual sex) is in the eye of the beholder."

H) Premature death from suicide:

"Luckily, I avoided it, but I thought about suicide a lot. I'd think about it and make myself sad over my premature death, and then I'd feel better."

Kaysen then compares herself with Daisy who did commit suicide at age 19:

"The idea of suicide worked on me like a purgative or a cathartic. For some people it's different -- Daisy, for instance. But was her death really 'premature'? Ought she to have sat in her eat-in kitchen with her chicken and her anger for another fifty years? I'm assuming she wasn't going to change, and I may be wrong..."

"I say to myself: Are you crazy? ...It means something particular to me: the tunnels, the security screens, the plastic forks, the shimmering, ever-shifting borderline that like all boundaries beckons and asks to be crossed. I do not want to cross it again."

CHAPTER 7: "GIRL, INTERRUPTED" -- SIGNIFICANCE

The implications and significance of Kaysen's Girl, Interrupted can be partly understood by considering the media reaction to her book. Here's a partial list of comments from reviews:

"...A minimalist relative of *One Flew Over the Cuckoo's Nest*, Kaysen's spare, elegant book raises angry questions about just who's crazy, and who's in charge of figuring it out."

--*Los Angeles Times Book Review*

"At turns wry, sardonic, witty... an unusual glimpse of a young woman's experience with insanity. Kaysen presents a meaningful analysis of the dual and contradictory nature of psychiatric hospitalization as both refuge and prison."

--*San Francisco Chronicle*

"Memorable and stirring... fascinating. A powerful examination not only of Kaysen's own imperfections but of those of the system that diagnosed her."

--*Vogue*

"'Girl, Interrupted' is a writer's book, crafted by an author of extraordinary acuteness and skill. Kaysen takes us across the boundaries of 'normalcy.' 'Girl, Interrupted' is about the borders between the world inside the hospital and the world outside, between sanity and insanity, between freedom and captivity, between self and other, between dignity and shame, between power and powerlessness."

-- *Boston Phoenix Literary Section*

"Using herself as a troubled -- and troubling -- example, Kaysen demonstrates with excoriating humor the severe problems with diagnosis, the phenomenon of psychiatric hospitalization and the callousness of even the most sophisticated of families and hospitals. 'Girl, Interrupted' is more than a '60s period piece. It is a cautionary tale for our time, for any era struggling to balance on the razor's edge between sanity and insanity."

--*St. Louis Post Dispatch*

"Susanna Kaysen's candid memoir of her stay in a psychiatric hospital breaks the mold. It is both funny and frightening. Kaysen's account is provocative, concise writing with an occasional edge of black humor. It makes us examine our own minds and wonder just who has the right to decide if someone has gone mad."

--*St. Petersburg Times*

Recent mass shootings including the Newtown, Conn. killings in December, 2012, have resulted in a re-examination of the U.S. mental health system, gun control, violence in films/TV/video games, etc.

Since the 1960s, civil libertarians, liberals, college professors, the media, and Hollywood movies and TV have pushed for the "constitutional rights" of the mentally ill who have been confined to mental institutions.

The civil libertarian activist movement against the mental health system since the 1960s has resulted in the elimination of nearly 95% of psychiatric beds -- mental hospitals have been closed, laws to involuntarily commit dangerous psychotics have been weakened or dropped, and psychotic mental patients have been released into the streets -- untreated, with no anti-psychotic medication.

Liberal activists claimed that somehow the mentally ill would find their way into half-way houses and then transition back to society by magic. The unintended consequences of this over-idealistic, activist, civil-libertarian crusade has resulted in dangerous, violent psychotics wandering the streets. Some of them have been guilty of mass shootings and killings.

R.D. Laing, the British psychiatrist, wrote that schizophrenia was a somewhat healthy reaction to the environment and that schizophrenics were having a mystical experience. He inspired Ken Kesey to write *One Flew Over the Cuckoo's Nest* which was made into an Academy Award winning film in 1975.

One Flew Over the Cuckoo's Nest -- Brief Synopsis:

When free-spirited petty crook Randle P. McMurphy (Jack Nicolson) arrives at the state mental hospital, his contagious sense of disorder jolts the routine. He's on one side of a brewing war, soft-spoken, coolly monstrous Nurse Ratched (Louise Fletcher) on the other. At stake is the fate of every patient on the ward.

The film is an electrifying adaptation of Ken Kesey's acclaimed bestseller which swept all five major 1975 Academy Awards. Raucous, searing and with a superb cast that includes Brad Dourif, Danny DeVito, and Christopher Lloyd in his film debut, it soars.

Who didn't want to free R.P. McMurphy (Jack Nicolson) after seeing the movie version of *One Flew Over the Cuckoo's Nest*? *Girl, Interrupted* is another book in the same anti-psychiatric hospital tradition.

Bernie Reeves, Editor and Publisher, *Raleigh Metro Magazine*, wrote in the *Wall Street Journal*, January, 2013:

How the Mentally Ill Were Released into U.S. Streets

"In response to your Dec. 26 editorial *Hard Newtown Questions*... Your stating the need to address the issue of the severely mentally ill is a view I have espoused for 30 years as a columnist in my regional magazine."

"I point to the fringe pop psychiatry experiments by British doctor R.D. Laing in 1950s and '60s that deified schizophrenics for their alleged mystical harmony with the universe. Laing switched roles between doctor and patient to make his point, inspiring author Ken Kesey to write One Flew Over the Cuckoo's Nest, his fictional homage to Laing. Kesey's hero is the schizophrenic R.P. McMurphy (Jack Nicolson), and the enemy is Nurse Ratched (Louise Fletcher), who represents the square world of sane people."

"The film of Kesey's book was a key element in selling the manifesto that the confinement of the mentally ill was a violation of their constitutional rights, adding propulsion to the movement to release the seriously mentally ill onto the streets of America. Their release was accompanied by the simultaneous eradication of loitering and vagrancy laws -- and complicity by the media, which characterized the phenomenon as the failure of the capitalism. The real truth eventually emerged but was minimally communicated to the public."

"As you point out in your editorial, after each massacre there is a call for swift justice followed by a shrill cry to ban guns, leaving the real problem of handling the mentally ill on the sidelines."

"I think this is due to the accumulation of identity-rights propaganda for the insane that causes the mass media to avoid pointing the finger for fear of violating the politically correct code that now impedes out public dialogue. With nowhere else to turn to display the proper outrage, the news industry goes back to gun control."

"Though I am not a gun fanatic, I feel the ridicule of the NRA for suggesting armed guards be posted at schools is unfair. Children are familiar with security -- airports, the mall, public buildings -- yet they are left exposed where they spend nearly every day, their schools. Many public schools already have police or security guards for other reasons, so why not protect the lives of students?"

I would disagree with diagnosing the R.P. McMurphy as "schizophrenic" -- he seems to be more of an antisocial personality disorder type. But the other points Reeves makes seem valid.

David Kopel, research director of the Independence Institute and co-author of the law school textbook, "Firearms Law and the Second Amendment", wrote an article which appeared in the *Wall Street Journal* on December 17, 2012 in reaction to the Newtown mass killings:

"Has the rate of random mass shootings in the United States increased? Over the past 30 years, the answer is definitely yes. It is also true that the total U.S. homicide rate has fallen by over half since 1980, and the gun homicide rate has fallen along with it. Today, Americans are safer from violent crime, including gun homicide, than they have been at any time since the mid-1960s."

I don't want to get off the spine of the story of BPD, but the issue of the general treatment of the mentally ill impacts people with Borderline Personality Disorder as well as other psychiatric disorders.

I'll just summarize Kopel's survey of gun control statistics which show:

"Since gun controls today are far stricter than at the time when 'active shooters' (criminals who attempt to murder people in a confined area, where there are lots of people, and who chose at least some victims randomly) were rare, what can account for the increase in these shootings?"

"One plausible answer is the media. Cable TV in the 1990s, and the Internet today, greatly magnify the instant celebrity that a mass killer can achieve. We know that many would-be mass killers obsessively study their predecessors."

"Loren Coleman's 2004 book "The Copycat Effect: How the Media and Popular Culture Trigger the Mayhem in Tomorrow's Headlines" shows that the copycat effect is as old as the media itself."

Kopel points out a second problem resulting from the excesses of the civil libertarian activists which I've been discussing:

"A second explanation is the deinstitution of the violently mentally ill. A 2000 *New York Times* study of 100 rampage murderers found that 47 were mentally ill. In the *Journal of the American Academy of Psychiatry Law* (2008), Jason C. Matejkowski and his co-authors reported that 16% of state prisoners who had perpetrated murders were mentally ill."

"In the mid-1960s, many of the killings would have been prevented because the severely mentally ill would have been confined and cared for in a state (mental) institution. But today, while government at most every level has bloated over the past half-century, mental-health treatment has been decimated. According to a study released in July by the Treatment Advocacy Center, the number of state hospital beds in America per capita has plummeted to 1850 levels, or 14.1 beds per 100,000 people."

"Moreover, a 2011 paper by Steven P. Segal at the University of California, Berkeley, 'Civil Commitment Law, Mental Health Services, and U.S. Homicide Rates,' found that a third of the state-to-state variation in homicide rates was attributable to the strength or weakness of involuntary civil-commitment laws."

Kopel discusses the problem of pretend "gun-free zones" vs. law abiding, armed adults. He closes with this warning:

"People who are serious about preventing the next Newtown should embrace much greater funding for mental health, strong laws for civil commitment of the violently mentally ill -- and stop kidding themselves that pretend gun-free zones will stop killers."

Dr. E. Fuller Torrey and Doris A. Fuller of the Treatment Advocacy Center, Arlington, Virginia, had an article published on Dec. 19, 2012 in *The Wall Street Journal*:

The Potential Killers We Let Loose

"The U.S. would have fewer mass killings if individuals with severe mental illnesses received proper treatment."

Gun Control vs. the Severely Mentally Ill:

"There are many good reasons to improve gun control in the United States, including the obscene firepower available in many weapons. But better gun control will do little to prevent many mass killings, such as occurred last week in Newtown, Conn. Even if you ban guns completely, there are many alternative weapons available for use by untreated severely mentally ill persons who are so inclined."

Knives vs. the Severely Mentally Ill:

"Knives, for example. One the same day Adam Lanza killed 20 children at Sandy Hook Elementary School in Connecticut, Min Yingjun stabbed 22 children at an elementary school in central China. Similar assaults using knives killed about 20 and wounded more than 50 children in China last year. Almost all the attacks were carried out by severely mentally ill men. So maybe we should ban knives."

Cars vs. the Severely Mentally Ill:

"What about cars? In 1989 Steven Abrams, diagnosed with schizophrenia, drove his car onto a school playground in California, killing two young children. He had been hospitalized for psychiatric problems and had talked of killing children. Also in California, Marie West, diagnosed with bipolar disorder and with 19 previous hospitalizations, intentionally ran over an elderly man in 2000."

"The following year David Attias, diagnosed with bipolar disorder and previously hospitalized, drove his car onto a sidewalk in the Golden State, killing four and injuring nine. He then got out of his car and said he was an 'angel of death.' Perhaps we should ban cars as well."

"The heart of this problem is not the availability of weapons but the abundance of individuals with severe mental disorders who are not being treated."

"Severe mental disorders are defined by the National Advisory Mental Health Council as including schizophrenia, schizoaffective disorders, bipolar disorder, autism and the severe forms of major depression, panic disorder, and obsessive-compulsive disorder. According to the National Institute of Mental Health, 7.7 million Americans currently qualify for the first three diagnoses, with 3.5 million of them receiving no treatment at any given time."

"Among this 3.5 million, approximately 10%, or 350,000 individuals, become societal problems because of their untreated severe mental illness. According to federal statistics or academic studies, they comprise one-third of the homeless population and one-fifth of the inmates of jails and prisons, and they are responsible for at least 10% of all homicides in the U.S."

"Many killings by individuals with severe mental illness are one tragic symptom of a much larger problem. Over the past half-century, the availability of public psychiatric beds in the U.S. has decreased to 43,000 from 559,000, even as the population has increased. When individuals with severe mental illnesses are hospitalized at all, they are not kept long enough to become stabilized because of the bed shortage. Many are eventually incarcerated for petty crimes or worse."

"A 2010 survey by the Treatment Advocacy Center reported that there are over three times more severely mentally ill individuals in jails and prisons than in hospitals. The problem is further exacerbated by state commitment laws that impede the hospitalization of those who resist treatment."

"At this time, Adam Lanza's psychiatric diagnosis is not publicly known. Published accounts suggest that he fits into the autism spectrum, and it is known that a small number of such individuals become violent as adults. Such individuals require medications to control their behavior."

"While it isn't yet known whether Lanza was being treated, it is known that Connecticut is among the worst states to seek such treatment. It has among the weakest involuntary treatment laws and is one of only six states that doesn't have a law permitting court-ordered 'assisted outpatient treatment' (AOT). In study after study, AOT has been shown to decrease re-hospitalizations, incarcerations and, most importantly, episodes of violence among severely mentally ill individuals."

"Would we have fewer mass killings in the U.S. if we made sure that individuals with severe mental illness were receiving treatment? Examining the other 10 largest mass killings suggests that answer is yes."

"Seung-Hui Cho, who killed 32 at Virginia Tech, Howard Unruh, who killed 13 in Camden, N.J.; and Jiverly Wong, who killed 13 in Binghamton, N.Y., all had untreated schizophrenia. James Holmes, who killed 12 in an Aurora, Colo., movie theater almost certainly was severely mentally ill, but clinical information has not yet been released."

"George Hennard, who killed 23 in a Killeen, Texas, cafeteria, had definite paranoid thinking. Patrick Sherill, who killed 14 in an Edmond, Okla., post office, was known as 'crazy Pat' by his neighbors but never formally diagnosed."

"By contrast, little or no evidence of severe mental illness exists for Eric Harris and Dylan Klebold, who killed 13 at a high school in Littleton, Colo.; James Huberrty, who killed 21 at a McDonald's in San Ysidro, Calif.; and U.S. Army Maj. Nidal Malik Hasan, who killed 13 at the Fort Hood military base in Texas. Yet Charles Whitman, who killed 14 in Austin, Texas, was found at autopsy to have a tumor in the part of the brain that controls aggression."

"It is now clearly established that people with severe mental illness who are being treated are no more dangerous than the general population. But some with severe illnesses who are not being treated are more dangerous. Therefore, if we ensure treatment for those who are known to be potentially dangerous, we may not eliminate mass killings but we would reduce them significantly. And perhaps if we had already done so, 20 small children in Newtown, Conn., might be alive today awaiting Christmas."

CHAPTER 8: "SINGLE WHITE FEMALE" & BPD

In the film, based on the book by John Lutz, *Single White Female*, the character of Hedy has been cited as an example of Borderline Personality Disorder (BPD).

She suffers from a markedly disturbed sense of identity, and tries to remedy it by adopting wholesale the attributes of her roommate. It is implied that she feels a deep-seated emptiness, while her fear of abandonment leads to drastic measures.

The ad: SWF seeks female to share apt in West 70s. Non-smoker, professional preferred...

An innocent want ad opens the door to murderous, unrelenting terror in this pulse-pounding psychological shocker starring Bridget Fonda and Jennifer Jason Leigh.

There is something odd about the way Hedra openly envies Allie's appearance and lifestyle. Then Allie begins receiving obscene phone calls from strangers who know her name; her credit cards mysteriously disappear; and she is shocked to discover that Hedra's wardrobe is eerily similar to her own.

Unknown to Allie, her plain and modest roommate is sharing much more than the rent...and an unspeakable, bloody nightmare is just beginning.,,

Allie's new roommate is about to borrow a few things... Her clothes. Her boyfriend. Her life.

Single White Female -- Plot:

Allison "Allie" Jones (Bridget Fonda) is a software designer in New York City, engaged to Sam Rawson (Steven

Weber). In the middle of the night, Sam's ex-wife calls, and it is revealed that he slept with her recently; Allie breaks off the engagement and asks him to leave.

The next morning she attends a business lunch with Mitchell Myerson (Stephen Tobolowsky), a fashion house owner who is looking to buy Allie's revolutionary new program. He manipulates her into significantly lowering the cost, on the basis that his recommendations within the industry will be her future business. As he is her first and only client, she accepts.

Allie advertises for a new roommate. She eventually settles on Hedra Carlson (Jennifer Jason Leigh), whom she decided to nickname "Hedy", and they become friends. Hedy tells how she was suppose to be a twin but her twin was stillborn, leaving her with a constant feeling of loneliness.

After a few weeks, however, Hedy reveals her true nature: secretive, manipulative and deeply disturbed. She erases Sam's phone messages when he calls to plead with Allie for a reconciliation, and takes a letter he sends for her. She secretly buys a puppy and pretends it was a stray in order to bond with Allie. Her behavior worsens when Sam returns in person and is able to win Allie back.

Fearing she will be kicked out of the apartment in favor of Sam, Hedy does everything possible to make Sam look bad, even killing the puppy and making it look like it was his fault. Hedy then copies Allie's appearance, right down to her hairstyle.

Myerson attempts to rape Allie on completion of their deal, insinuating that if she does not submit to him, he will warn off future clients and not pay her. She fights back and escapes.

Allie finds a box in Hedy's room containing Sam's letter, Hedy's real name (Ellen Besch), and newspaper clippings revealing her twin sister actually drowned when they were nine. She follows an unaware Hedy that night to an underground sex club, and witnesses her passing herself off as Allie.

Utterly disturbed, she seeks out her friend Graham, who insists she get Hedy to move out. Hedy overhears their conversation and later attacks Graham.

Hedy, posing as Allie, sneaks into Sam's hotel room and performs oral sex on him. Afterwards Hedy attempts to blackmail Sam but he insists on telling Allie the truth. Hedy kills him by gouging his eye with her stiletto heel. As she leaves his apartment complex, the doorman mistakes her for Allie.

The next day Hedy tells Allie she is about to leave. Later Allie sees a news report on Sam's death, realizes what has happened and tries to leave. Hedy takes Allie hostage at gunpoint. She states she intends to frame Allie for Sam's murder since any witnesses will assume they are the same person, forcing Allie to run away with her in order to evade arrest.

As Myerson did not make the full payment to Allie, her anti-theft software activates and erases his files. He comes to the apartment building looking for Allie and, finding her tied up, attempts to free her.

Before he can set her free, however, Hedy sneaks up on him and kills him. A violent fight ensues, during which Graham regains consciousness and is able to briefly assist Allie. The struggle ends with Allie stabbing Hedy to death.

In an epilogue, Allie narrates that she has finally moved on. She forgives Hedy for killing Sam, and herself for killing Hedy, as she believes Hedy's downfall was an example of how survivor's guilt can destroy someone. The film ends with a closeup of a photograph presumably made by Hedy of their faces superimposed into one, it lies partly hidden from view amongst Allie's possessions.

Hedy & Criteria for BPD:

1) Unclear & unstable self-concept -- Hedy exudes self-disdain, idealizes Allie's looks and lifestyle. Hedy fixes her hair like Allies, dyes it reddish, dresses exactly like Allie. She poses as Allie to commit crimes. She uses a false name from the start of the story. Lies about her background and family.

2) Worries about abandonment -- Hedy freaks out when Allie makes-up with her ex-boyfriend because she fears she'll be alone, no longer Allie's roommate.

When Hedy tastes mini-abandonment when Allie spends a night with her boyfriend without telling Hedy, she's furious, rants and raves at Allie when she comes home the next night. Frantic, drastic measures include killing a puppy and blaming it on Allie's boyfriend, then several murders to cover her tracks.

3) Hedy impulsively engages in sensation seeking behavior including sexual acting out at an underground sex club posing as Allie. Then having sex with Allie's boyfriend in a dark room, posing as Allie with Allie's hairstyle, clothes, perfume.

4) Roller coaster emotions characterize Hedy's fragmented personality -- Allie stays out with her boyfriend, Hedy

goes into deep despair, for example. She gets into a rage because Allie wants to get rid of her as a roommate.

5) Explosiveness -- Hedy shows dramatic bouts of rage, anger, and violence over minor problems. Most people with roommate problems just change roommmates. For Hedy this is a life-and-death issue -- when Allie and her friends want to reject Hedy, Hedy's solution is murder.

6) Emptiness -- Hedy acts like she's an empty shell and she needs to fill herself out by imitating and clinging to Allie. She says Allie is in a different league with great style vs. Hedy's a loser from her own viewpoint.

7) Up-and-down relationships -- Allie experiences emotional whiplash from Hedy's frequent changes from idolization of Allie to demonization of her. When Allie discovers Hedy's family contact phone and calls them, her father calls, Hedy answers and tells him never to call again. She says they want to put her away in a mental hospital.

8) Dissociation -- Hedy feels out of touch with reality. She suffers from intense, unwarranted mistrust of others initially. Then Hedy sets herself up to be rejected, begins murdering people, and ultimately is killed when Allie fights back in self-defense.

9) Self-harm -- Hedy's BPD symptoms lead to her downfall and death. She's very self-destructive while attempting to avoid initial abandonment. Her drastic measures to hurt and kill others leads to her own destruction.

Hedy seems to not only have five or more symptoms of BPD but all nine of them.

CHAPTER 9: "THE ROOMMATE" & BPD

The Rebecca character in the thriller movie, The Roommate, portrays a Borderline Personality Disorder (BPD) type similar to the Hedy character in *Single White Female*.

Rebecca's cute. She's loyal. She's psychotic. And, unfortunately for college freshman Sara, she's THE ROOMMATE. When Sara arrives at school, she finds new romance with Stephen and forms a fast friendship with her new roommate Rebecca.

What begins as camaraderie soon turns creepy, and Sara comes face to face with the terrifying realization that her new best friend is obsessive, unbalanced... and maybe even a killer!

Murder can really ruin a friendship.

The Roommate -- Plot:

Sara Matthews (Minka Kelly) is starting her freshman year of college in L.A. She meets Tracy (Aly Michalka), Stephen (Cam Gigandet), her love interest, and Rebecca (Leighton Meester), her roommate.

Initially, the girls begin to bond and Rebecca learns that Sara had an older sister, Emily, who died when Sara was nine. Sara has Emily's name tattooed on her body. She also has an ex-boyfriend, Jason (Matt Lanter), who keeps calling her to try to reconcile.

As time goes on, Rebecca's obsession with Sara escalates which causes her to become increasingly violent. And then Rebecca tries to drive away anyone who could come between them.

Rebecca attacks Tracy in the shower and threatens to kill her unless she stays away from Sara. Tracy moves to another dorm, fearful of Rebecca.

And old friend of Sara named Irene, who is also a lesbian, invites her to move in with them, but when Sara tells that to Rebecca, she plans to insure that Sara will stay with her by taking Sara's pet kitten, Cuddles, and puts him in a dryer (offscreen).

Rebecca lies to Sara and tells her that the kitten ran away. When Sara's philandering fashion design professor (Billy Zane) kisses her, Rebecca plans to get the professor out of the picture to impress Sara by seducing him. Rebecca records their dialogue on a tape recorder to make it look like he was sexually abusing her.

Later Rebecca lies once again to Sara, telling her she went looking for Cuddles, claiming she was raped and beaten brutally by a street thug. In reality, the wounds on Rebecca's body are self-inflicted. Sara feels bad for her and decides to spend Thanksgiving with Rebecca.

During her stay, Sara overhears a conversation between Rebecca and her father (David Patrick Kelly), hinting Rebecca has had trouble making friends in the past.

Rebecca's mother (Frances Fisher) mentions that Rebecca is suppose to be taking medication.

Later, Sara and Rebecca encounter Maria (Nina Dobrev), an old friend of Rebecca's to whom Sara bares a striking resemblance. Sara and Stephen later find a bottle of Zyprexa pills, which they find out (via Wikipedia) is used to treat schizophrenia and bipolar disorder.

But the bottle is full, implying that Rebecca didn't take any pills. Sara, worried what would happen, decides to move in with Irene. Irene (Danneel Harris) goes to a club where she sees Rebecca.

They make out in the club's bathroom and Irene, not knowing that Rebecca is Sara's roommate, goes back to her place. The following morning, Sara goes to Irene's place but she's not there.

Rebecca gets Sara's sister's name tattooed in the same place on her body as Sara, saying that Sara can now think of Rebecca as her sister. A shocked Sara realizes that Rebecca is obsessed with her, packs all her things, except her sister's necklace which she can't find. It is later revealed that the necklace had been stolen from Sara by Rebecca.

Jason arrives at Sara's dorm and slips a note under her door, saying that he wants to see her. Rebecca reads the note, impersonates Sara with her sister's necklace and tattoo, and dyes her hair to look like Sara. She then goes to Jason's hotel room and stabs him.

Later, Sara gets a text from Irene, saying she needs her right away. Sara informs Stephen she will be at Irene's place. When she gets there, she finds Irene held hostage by Rebecca with a pistol.

Rebecca reveals that she was responsible for what happened to Tracy, Cuddles, the professor, and Jason. Sara says she did it all to win Sara's friendship.

When Sara apologizes, Rebecca forgives her, but wants to kill Irene in order to finally have Sara all to herself. Stephen arrives just in time to help stop Rebecca from pulling the trigger on Irene.

In the ongoing struggle, Stephen is knocked unconscious and Sara is left dangling out of the window. Although Rebecca pulls Sara back to safety, Sara reaches for the pistol to shoot Rebecca, knowing how homicidal she is. She knows Rebecca will continue to harm others close to Sara.

However, the gun is empty. Enraged at this, Rebecca picks up Sara and attempts to squeeze her to death. But Sara stabs Rebecca in the back with a boxcutter, whispering "You were never my friend." And kills her.

Sara moves back into her dorm and moves the extra bed out of her room, proclaiming that she does not want a roommate for a while.

The Roommate -- Reviews:

The consensus on the "Rotten Tomatoes" website, based on 81 reviews, is that "*The Roommate* is devoid of chills, thrills, or even cheap titillation -- *The Roommate* isn't even bad enough to be good."

Keith Staskiewicz of Entertainment Weekly gave *The Roommate* a low rating, saying it "is really just a far-below-par thriller that desperately wishes it were a different movie -- a longing it shares with the audience. He praised Meester for bringing "the slightest trace of something fascinating to her role. When she smiles, it's perfectly located between a sweet display of affection and a snarling warning."

Peter Travers of *Rolling Stone* gave it a half star, stating that "*The Roommate* -- the umpteenth uncredited remake of 1992's Single White Female -- sucks bad, real bad" and that "Danish director Christian E. Christiansen has no flair for suspense."

Meester's performance garnered praise from other top critics, including the *Los Angeles Times*, which states: "Here her performance often has the feeling of a sports car in neutral. When she punches it for quick changes of tone from manic to wounded or around the bend, she shows how much more she is capable of."

Chicago Sun-Times film critic Roger Ebert called Leighton Meester's character "A combination between Lindsay Lohan and Amy Fisher."

Rebecca & BPD:

Rebecca in *The Roommate*, like similar BPD characters (such as in *Single White Female*, *Fatal Attraction*, *Play Misty for Me*), shows symptoms of Borderline Personality Disorder:

1) Panic about abandonment -- Rebecca kills to keep Sara as a roommate and friend. She goes to drastic measures over fears about abandonment.

2) Impulsivity -- sensation seeking: Rebecca does some sexual acting out and a lot of reckless behavior in her sick obsession over Sara.

3) Yo-yo emotions: Rebecca experiences a roller coaster of emotional swings. When she thinks things are going her way with Sara, she's on a high. But her emotions flip-flop to highly anxious and distressed at seemingly trivial triggers.

4) Explosiveness: Rebecca gets into extreme rages when she's threatened by others getting close to Sara. For instance, she angrily beats-up and threatens another girl in the dorm who is too friendly with Sara; Rebecca murders Sara's ex-boyfriend when he comes to town.

5) Unstable self-concept: Rebecca tries to bond with Sara by getting the same tattoo, wears her necklace, and stalks her. Rebecca has no clear sense of values or purpose other than to haunt Sara.

6) Emptiness: Rebecca feels empty inside and aims to fill herself by attaching to Sara, sexually acting-out, etc.

7) Up-and-down relationships: Rebecca rapidly puts Sara, her new love, on a pedestal; then her pedestal collapses with the slightest disappointment. One minute Rebecca is idolizing Sara and the next minute she's demonizing her.

8) Dissociation -- feeling out of touch with reality: Rebecca suffers from unwarranted mistrust of others, especially those who want to share Sara with her.

9) Self-harm: While Rebecca is not suicidal, her self-destructive stalking of and obsession with Sara leads to

her own death. So her conduct is in effect suicidal over time.

CHAPTER 10: "THE CRUSH" & BPD

In the thriller film, *The Crush*, the character Adrian, a 14-year-old girl, has Borderline Personality Disorder.

The Crush -- Plot:

Arriving in a new city, writer Nick Eliot (Cary Elwes) secures a job at *Pique* magazine and lodgings in a guest house belonging to Cliff and Liv Forrester (Kurtwood Smith and Gwynyth Walsh).

The handsome Nick soon makes the acquaintance of the Forrester's teenage daughter, Adrian (Alicia Silverstone), a precocious, gifted girl who has Borderline Personality Disorder.

Adrian develops an intense attraction to Nick. She secretly helps Nick by sneaking into his room and rewriting one of his *Pique* stories, which subsequently wins a rave from his editor/boss Michael (Matthew Walker).

At a party thrown by the Forresters, Nick agrees to accompany the lonely girl on a nighttime drive to a romantic spot where she kisses him. This intensifies Adrian's crush on Nick, but he quickly wises up and attempts to put her off, having begun a budding romance with co-worker Amy (Jennifer Rubin).

Adrian continues to boldly pursue him, even going so far as to undress in his view. Nick, however, continues to rebuff her advances, and Adrian's stalking actions become destructive. She defaces a car he's restored and erases his computer discs -- yet he's unable to convince her parents, Cliff and Liv, of what's going on.

Cheyenne (Amber Benson), a friend of Adrian who tries to warn Nick about her, meets with an "accident" at the riding school they attend together. Then, after Adrian spies on Amy in bed with Nick, the girl locks Amy in her darkroom and empties a wasps' nest into the vents.

Amy survives, and Nick, now convinced that Adrian is big trouble, attempts to find new housing. However, Adrian manages to sabotage his efforts. She then accuses him of sexually assaulting her with "evidence" obtained from a used condom from Nick's trash, leading to his arrest.

After Michael bails him out and fires him, Nick is met once again by Cheyenne. She informs Nick that she knows he did not do anything to Adrian. She tells him Adrian behaved like this before to a previous crush, a camp counselor named Rick who "accidentally" died by eating something poisonous.

Cheyenne also informs Nick of a diary Adrian kept that can acquit him. When Cheyenne leaves, Nick goes looking for her when he hears strange noises from Forresters' house. He discovers Cheyenne tied up in the attic and is confronted by Adrian and then Cliff who attacks him.

Adrian, still infatuated, attacks her father, leaving Nick free to subdue her with one punch. Acquitted, Nick goes to live with Amy while Adrian, confined to a psychiatric ward, wishes to express her remorse for what she has done to Nick. Her doctor comments that she is making good progress, but seems to be yet unaware she is developing a crush on him.

Adrian's BPD symptoms:

1) Adrian takes frantic actions to avoid abandonment by her love object, Nick. She attacks his girlfriend, Amy.

2) Unstable interpersonal relationships -- Cheyenne verifies that Adrian has stalked and murdered at least one prior crush, poisoned a camp counselor.

3) Identity disturbance -- Adrian's unstable, fractured sense of self draws her to stalk her crush.

4) Impulsivity problems of Adrian include sexual acting-out and destructive behavior.

5) Affective instability -- Adrian panics when Nick gets close to Amy.

6) Chronic feelings of emptiness -- Adrian tries to fill the empty hole inside her by stalking, idolizing Nick.

7) Inappropriate, intense anger centering around Nick when he's pushing her away or with Amy.

8) Transient, stress related paranoid ideation or severe dissociative symptoms lead Adrian to assault and murder.

9) Adrian's obsessive stalking results in a suicidal path as she murders and puts her own life in danger.

CHAPTER 11: "MAD LOVE" & BPD

In the offbeat romance movie, *Mad Love*, Casey Roberts, the female lead has Borderline Personality Disorder.

Mad Love -- Plot:

In Seattle, straight-laced Matt Leland (Chris O'Donnell) falls in love with Casey Roberts (Drew Barrymore), the new girl at their high school who is from Chicago. They begin a sexual relationship.

His father disapproves of this and her parents try to stop the young couple from continuing to see each other. She deliberately sets off the fire alarm at school, knowing that there is no fire there, and is subsequently suspended from school.

She has an argument with her parents when they tell her they are sending her to a boarding school. She takes an overdose and her parents subsequently arrange to have her committed.

He helps her escape from an acute psychiatric ward, and as they run away they both deal with her Borderline Personality Disorder.

Casey is eccentric in nature. Her impulsiveness and extreme risk-taking attitude and behavior is attributed to her illness, in which she experiences severe highs and lows of emotion. Her frequent intense feelings, of passion towards Matt and of fear and destructiveness, dominate her persona.

Throughout the relationship, Matt selflessly puts her needs before his. The severity of this increases as her mental state worsens.

Heading toward Mexico in his SUV, Casey becomes increasingly reckless and over-emotional. They crash and abandon the vehicle. They hitchhike, accepting a lift from a salesman (Liev Schreiber). He puts his hand on her crotch, she puts her lit cigarette against his face. He throws her out and a fight ensues between him and Matt.

The couple steal his car and continue their journey. She becomes more distressed and he does his best to help her. He becomes scared. She threatens suicide.

Casey also threatens to kill him with a gun she took from the glove compartment in the salesman's car. They return to Seattle and their families. She is readmitted to the psychiatric hospital.

He goes home and much later receives a letter from her telling him she has moved back to Chicago and now feels significantly better. She says she has good memories of their time together.

Casey's BPD symptoms:

1) Casey has a pattern of sensation seeking, impulsivity. She gets sexually involved with Matt while her parents are against the relationship. She takes off for Mexico with Matt, recklessly crashes the car, hitchhikes, fights with a driver and steals his car.

2) Self-harm -- Casey takes a suicidal overdose and is committed to a psychiatric hospital.

3) Labile affect, yo-yo emotions -- Casey goes through highs and lows, love and hate frequently.

4) Explosiveness -- Casey gets into sudden bouts of anger, rage. She sets off a fire alarm in high school and is suspended.

5) Unstable self-concept -- Casey argues with her parents because they plan to send her to a boarding school and takes an overdose. She has self-disdain, gets very depressed, and suicidal.

6) Casey feels an emptiness -- a black hole within. She tries to fill it up with a love affair with Matt, escapes to Mexico on a reckless trip.

7) Up-and-down relationships -- Casey loves Matt but shuffles through all kinds of feelings from love to hate. She threatens to kill him with a gun in Mexico.

8) Dissociation -- feeling out of touch with reality. Casey flips out, suffers from intense mistrust of others at times. She loses touch with reality.

Mad Love -- reception:

Critic Emanuel Levy wrote a mixed review of *Mad Love* in *Variety*. He labeled the film as "yet another variation on amour fou and love-on-the-run that makes little sense and fails to reach the heart." But he also commented that *Mad Love* presents a "realistic portrayal of mental illness."

CHAPTER 12: "THE CABLE GUY" & BPD

The Cable Guy, Ernie "Chip" Douglas, has Borderline Personality Disorder.

The Cable Guy -- Plot:

After a failed marriage proposal to his girlfriend Robin Harris (Leslie Mann), Steven M. Kovacs (Matthew Broderick) moves into his own apartment after they agree to spend some time apart.

Enthusiastic cable guy Ernie "Chip" Douglas (Jim Carrey), a man with a lisp, installs his cable. Taking advice from his friend Rick (Jack Black), Steven bribes Chip to give him free movie channels, to which Chip agrees. Before he leaves, Chip gets Steven to hang out with him the next day and makes him one of his "preferred customers".

As promised, Chip arrives the next day. He takes Steven to the satellite dish responsible for sending out television. Steven tells his problems with Robin to Chip, who tells him to admit his faults to Robin. Chip advises him to invite her over to watch *Sleepless in Seattle*, which is running on HBO the next night.

Steven takes Chip's advice, and Robin agrees to watch the movie with him. The next day, Chip begins acting more suspicious, "running into" Steven and his friends at the gym and leaving 10 messages on Steven's answering machine.

When Robin arrives to watch the movie, the cable is out, thanks to Chip, who intentionally sabotaged Seven's cable when he didn't call Chip back. Chip fixes the cable under the condition that they hang out again. Steven agrees.

The next evening, Chip takes Steven to *Medieval Times*, where Chip arranges for them to battle in the arena, referencing the Star Trek episode "Amok Time". Chip behaves aggressively, nearly killing Steven, who eventually bests him in combat.

Afterwards, Chip congratulates Steven, who decides the experience was fun. When they arrive at Steven's home, Chip reveals that he's installed an expensive home theater system in is living room.

Chip and Steven later host a party complete with a karaoke sing-off. With Chip's help, Steven sleeps with a woman named Heather, while Chip serenades the party singing Jefferson Airplane's *Somebody to Love*. The next morning Chip reveals that Heather ia a prostitute. Furious, Seven throws Chip out. Chip tells Steven he will make things better.

Chip tracks down Robin, who is on a date with another man (Owen Wilson). When the man goes to the bathroom, Chip beats him up and tells him to stay away from Robin. He later upgrades Robin's cable, saying that it's on Steven.

Robin decides to get back together with Steven as a result. Steven tells Chip that they cannot be friends, which hurts Chip. Chip then begins a series of vengeful acts.

He gets Steven arrested for possession of stolen property (the home theater system), although Steven is released on bail. Steven is later fired from his job when Chip sends out a video of Steven insulting his boss to the entire office that was recorded by hidden cameras in his apartment.

During a dinner with his family and Robin, Steven is horrified to see Chip is in attendance as well. Steven tells him to leave. But Chip tells him to play along or he will show everybody the picture of him with the prostitute.

The evening goes from bad to worse as Chip gets on well with Steven's family and leads everyone in a game of "porno password". Steven finally punches Chip when he implies he slept with Robin.

Rick later tells Steven that Chip has been fired from the cable company for stalking customers, and uses the names of television characters as aliases. Chip calls Steven that night, telling him he's paying Robin a visit. Steven tracks them down to the satellite dish, where Chip holds Robin hostage.

After a physical altercation and a chase, Steven gets the upper hand and he is able to save Robin. As the police arrive, Chip goes into a long speech on how he was raised on television ("I learned the facts of life by watching *The Facts of Life*!") and apologizes to Steven for being a bad friend.

He then dives into the satellite dish, which knocks out the cable across the entire town, just as the verdict in a highly publicized case involving a famous child star is about to be revealed. The following scene shows a man turning off his television and picking up a book, noticeably intrigued.

Chip survives the fall, but injures his back. As Steven and Robin reunite, Steven forgives Chip and asks for his real name. Chip jokingly replies "Ricky Ricardo". Chip is later taken to the hospital in a helicopter.

When one of the paramedics addresses him as "buddy", Chip asks the paramedic if he is truly his buddy, to which the paramedic replies, "Sure," causing Chip to smile deviously just before the credits roll.

MALICIOUS & BPD

The film *Malicious* (1995) presents a medical student with Borderline Personality Disorder. She's obsessed with her school's star baseball player, pursues him and finally manages to get him to spend the weekend with her.

However, when he soon returns to his girlfriend, her anger at his "betrayal" causes her to go over the edge. She places both her ex-lover's and his girlfriend's lives in danger.

STAR WARS & BPD

In the film *Star Wars*, Darth Vader (born Anakin Skywalker) is the central character of the *Star Wars* saga, appearing as one of the main antagonists of the original trilogy and as the main protagonist of the prequel trilogy. Darth Vader/Anakin Skywalker has Borderline Personality Disorder.

Darth Vader's iconic status has made the character a synonym for evil in popular culture, some psychiatrists have even considered him as a useful example to explain Borderline Personality Disorder to medical students.

Eric Bui, a psychiatrist at University of Toulouse Hospital, argued at the 2007 American Psychiatric Association convention that Anakin meets six of the nine diagnostic criteria for BPD, one more than necessary for a diagnosis of Borderline Personality Disorder.

He and a colleague, Rachel Rodgers, published their findings in a 2010 letter to the editor of the journal *Psychiatry Research*. Bui says he found Anakin Skywalker a useful example to explain BPD to medical students. In particular, Bui points to Anakin's:

1) abandonment issues

2) uncertainty over his identity

Anakin's mass murders of the Tusken Raiders in *Attack of the Clones* and the young Jedi in *Revenge of the Sith* count as:

3) two dissociative episodes

Bui hoped his paper would help raise awareness of the disorder, especially among teens.

CHAPTER 13: "NOTES ON A SCANDAL," "INTERIORS" & BPD

Two dramatic films, *Notes on a Scandal* and *Interiors*, show characters with Borderline Personality Disorder. In *Notes on a Scandal*, Sheba has BPD. *Interiors* showcases Eve who has BPD.

Notes on a Scandal -- Plot:

Barbara (Judi Dench), a veteran faculty member at a comprehensive school in London is neither a reliable nor disinterested first-person narrator in the story. A lonely, unmarried woman in her early sixties, she is eager to find a special, close friend.

However, she reveals that she has been unable to make a previous friendship last as she was accused of being domineering and demanding. Her former friend, teacher Jennifer Dodd, even threatened her with an injunction if she tried contacting her again.

When Bathsheba "Sheba" Hart (Cate Blanchett) is hired as an art teacher, Barbara immediately senses that they might become close friends. When Sheba invites Barbara for Sunday lunch with her family, she is ecstatic and gives the lunch date enormous significance.

Initially unknown to Barbara, Sheba falls in love with a 15-year-old pupil, Steven Connolly, who is from a deprived background and has literacy problems. Although they frequently have sex right from the start of their relationship, including at school and in the open on Hampstead Heath, the unlikely couple successfully conceal their affair from colleagues and family.

During Barbara's first visit to Sheba's residence, she tells Barbara a highly expurgated version of what has happened between her and Connolly, claiming only that he has tried to kiss her and that she discouraged his advances. Barbara offers her some advice on how to cool the boy's ardour, and considers the matter closed.

Sheba confesses to Barbara that despite her apparently charmed life, she feels unfulfilled. Sheba has a difficult relationship with her rebellious seventeen-year-old daughter, Polly, whose youth and beauty only intensify her mother's own feelings of aging and waste.

Sheba's husband, Richard, is significantly older than she is, and their relationship sometimes has a father-daughter feel to it. Sheba's complaints trouble Barbara, who had idealized Sheba and her family.

Barbara eventually finds out about the affair on Guy Fawkes Night, when she sees Sheba talking to Connolly on Primrose Hill. Barbara feels betrayed that Sheba did not confide in her during the early stages of their friendship, and is angered by Sheba's obsession with Connolly and her relative neglect of their friendship.

The power dynamics in the relationship between Connolly and Sheba are changing, with Connolly's interest in the affair waning as Sheba's grows. Sheba becomes needier and starts to write love letters to the boy. Connolly rejects Sheba when she visits his parents' council house, yet she does not break off the affair.

Some weeks after Sheba's confession, Brian Bangs, a mathematics teacher, asks Barbara to have Saturday lunch with him. He confesses his infatuation with Sheba, leading Barbara to realize that he is using her as a means to discover information about her private life.

Overcome with jealousy, Barbara alludes to Sheba's secret ("Sheba likes younger man, you know. *Much* younger men...

I mean you *are* aware of her *unusually* close relationship with one of the Year Eleven boys?").

Afterwards, Barbara is wracked with guilt, but cannot summon up the courage to tell Sheba what she has done. Rather, she hopes Bangs will not report what she has told him.

Sheba's relationship with Polly deteriorates further when the girl's unruly behavior results in her expulsion from her boarding school. On two occasions, Polly accuses Sheba of having an affair. Sheba is furious about the accusation, believing that she has covered her tracks successfully.

The school's headmaster is somehow informed about the illicit affair -- it is implied that the culprit is Bangs. Sheba is suspended from her job and charged with indecent assault on a pupil.

Her husband demands that she leave the family home and prevents her from seeing their children, especially their son Ben, who has Down's syndrome. Polly, meanwhile, refuses to have any contact with her.

While Sheba's life is quickly disintegrating, Barbara thrives on the new situation, which she considers her chance to prove her qualities as a friend, even when the headmaster, glad to rid himself of one of his severest critics, forces her into early retirement. Barbara gives up the lease on her own small flat and moves with Sheba into temporary accommodation in Sheba's brother's house.

Sheba finds Barbara's manuscript and discovers she has been writing an account of her relationship with Connolly. She is distraught and furious, not least because Barbara has written about events she did not personally witness, and made judgments about people close to Sheba. The film (and the novel it is based on) ends with Sheba, trapped and demoralized, resigning herself to Barbara's presence in her life.

Interiors -- Plot:

Three sisters, Renata (Diane Keaton), Flyn (Kristin Griffith), and Joey (Mary Beth Hurt) live through the painful separation of their parents.

Their father, Arthur (E.G. Marshall), parts from their controlling and mentally unstable but artistically inclined mother, Eve (Geraldine Page), going on to marry a more "normal" but plainer woman, Pearl (Maureen Stapleton).

The evening after Arthur marries Pearl, Eve commits suicide by walking into the ocean.

Confrontation between Eve vs. Arthur:

Here's part of a scene between Arthur and Eve when Eve realizes Arthur is divorcing her to marry another woman:

(Interior: Candlelit cathedral -- they walk down the aisle of an immense church)

Arthur: I think we should finalize our divorce.

Eve: (Looking away from Arthur) You do?

Arthur: Yeah, I think sooner or later we've got to... face reality and try to make new lives for ourselves.

Eve: You know it's very funny, because I thought that's what might be on your mind.

Arthur: It's not the end of the world.

Eve: (Her voice quavering) It's not? I think it's pretty goddamn terrible.

Arthur: Now, Eve, everything's going to be just fine.

Eve: (Her hand on her forehead, trying to gain control) Oh, I know that it's a little... soon perhaps to talk about a reconciliation, but I don't see why we have to finalize a divorce. I don't see why we can't just go on the way we are.

Arthur: W-we should each of us be free to make other plans.

Eve: Like what, what kind of plans?

Arthur: Well, in the event that... we meet other people--

Eve: (Interrupting) Oh!

Arthur: --become involved.

Eve: (Her voice rising) Well, what are you saying? You want to re-marry, is that it?

Arthur: I'm not discussing that.

Eve: Have you met someone?

Arthur: No.

Eve: Ooh, you're lying. Of course you've met someone. Why don't you be honest about it?

Arthur: Yes, I have, but you're going to make much too much out of it.

Eve: (Standing up) Oh, never mind, just don't talk anymore about it. I don't want to hear any more. (She walks to the front of the altar, where many red candles burn in their holders; Arthur follows her.)

Arthur: I talked with your doctor. He feels you can handle this.

Eve: You've talked to Dr. Lobell about this behind my back?

Arthur: Not behind your back. Discreetly.

Eve: (Putting her hand to her head) You've discussed this with Dr. Lobell... behind my back. It's so humiliating.

Arthur: Now, Eve, it's your doctor and myself. Now, how private can one be?

Eve: (Sighing, looking at Arthur) And he assured you that I can handle this. Is that what he-- H-h-how humiliating.

Arthur: You're not humiliated.

Eve: (Putting her hand to her face) Oh!! I just want to die!

Arthur: Now, stop that!

Eve: (Sighing) I just hate myself...! (She swoops her arm across the burning candles, smashing them off the altar, amid the harsh sound of breaking glass, Arthur grabs Eve's arm and pulls her away from the altar. Arthur puts his arm around Eve's waist and begins pulling her out of the dark cathedral, their voices trailing after them.)

Eve: I'm fine... I'm fine. (Arthur mumbles, desperately trying to hurry Eve out of the church) Oh, I hate myself, I hate myself, oh no!

Eve's BPD:

Some of Eve's BPD symptoms include self-harm (she commits suicide), roller coaster emotions, emptiness, and panic over abandonment.

CHAPTER 14: "THE CATCHER IN THE RYE" & BPD

In the novel *The Catcher in the Rye*, Holden Caulfield, the lead character appears to fit the Borderline Personality Disorder diagnosis.

The Catcher in the Rye -- Outline of Key Aspects:

In J.D. Salinger's *The Catcher in the Rye*, Holden Caulfield recounts the days following his expulsion from Pencey Prep, a private school.

After a fight with his roommate, Stradlater, Holden leaves school two days early to explore New York before returning home, interacting with teachers, prostitutes, nuns, an old girlfriend, and his sister along the way.

J.D. Salinger's classic, coming-of-age novel, *The Catcher in the Rye* illustrates a teenager's dramatic struggle against death and growing up.

The setting is Agerstown, Pennsylvania and NYC/Manhattan, 1950s. The main characters are Holden Caulfield, Phoebe, Allie, D.B., Mr. Antolini. The major thematic topics include innocence, death, authentic versus artificial, and sexual confusion. The major symbols include preparatory school life, a baseball glove, red hunting cap, Radio City Music Hall, the carrousel's gold ring, and the coming-of-age genre.

Important aspects of *The Catcher in the Rye*:

1) Holden Caulfield is one of the best-loved fictional characters in American literature. Like another popular character, Huck Finn, Holden tells his own story in his own words as if speaking aloud, and it is Holden's "voice" on the page, rather than the plot of *The Catcher in the Rye*, for which the novel is most remembered.

2) Although The Catcher in the Rye seems like the unedited thoughts and feelings of an actual teenager, it is nothing of the kind. Actually, J.D. Salinger was in his twenties and thirties when he wrote the novel, which began as a short story and grew, over the years, into a book length work of fiction.

3) The novel's main thematic conflict pits the innocence and authenticity of childhood, as represented by Holden's sister Phoebe, against the phoniness, as Holden sees it, of most adults (Mr. Antolini, for example). Neither a child nor a grownup, Holden resists maturation, a process he sees as characterized by loss rather than growth.

4) Holden Caulfield, the seventeen-year-old narrator and protagonist of the novel, addresses the reader directly from a mental hospital or sanitarium in southern California. Holden begins by saying:

"If you really want to hear about it, the first thing you'll probably want to know is where I was born, and what my lousy childhood was like, and how my parents were occupied and all before they had me, and all that David Copperfield kind of crap, but I don't feel like going into it, if you want to know the truth..."

He wants to tell us about events that took place over a two-day period the previous December.

Typically, he first digresses to mention his older brother, D.B., who was once a "terrific" short-story writer but now has sold out and writes scripts in nearby Hollywood.

On D.B.:

"...Now he's out in Hollywood, D.B., being a prostitute. If there's one thing I hate, it's the movies. Don't even mention them to me..."

The body of the novel follows. It is a *frame story*, or long flashback, constructed through Holden's memory.

5) Holden begins at Pencey Prep, an exclusive private school in Pennsylvania,

On the Saturday afternoon of the traditional football game with school rival, Saxon Hall. Holden misses the game.

Holden complains about a lack of girls at the game:

"There were never many girls at all at the football games. Only seniors were allowed to bring girls with them... I like to be somewhere at least where you can see a few girls around once in a while, even if they're only scratching their arms or blowing their noses or even just giggling or something."

"Old Selma Thurmer -- she was the headmaster's daughter -- showed up at the games quite often, but she wasn't exactly the type that drove you mad with desire. She was a pretty nice girl, though. I sat next to her once in the bus from Agerstown and we sort of struck up a conversation. I liked her."

"She had a big nose and her nails were all bitten down and bleedy-looking and she had on those damn falsies that point all over the place, but you felt sort of sorry for her. What I liked about her, she didn't give you a lot of horse manure about what a great guy her father was. She probably knew what a phony slob he was."

Manager of the fencing team, he managed to lose the team's equipment on the subway that morning, resulting in the cancellation of a match in New York.

He is on his way to the home of his history teacher, Mr. Spencer, to say good-bye. Holden has been expelled and is not to return after Christmas break, which begins Wednesday.

6) Spencer is a well-meaning but long-winded old man, and Holden gladly escapes to the quiet of an almost deserted dorm. Wearing his new red hunting cap, he begins to read. His reverie is temporary.

First, a dorm neighbor named Ackley disturbs him:

"...about eighty-five times a day old Ackley barged in on me. He was probably the only guy in the whole dorm, besides me, that wasn't down at the game... He was a very peculiar guy... He was one of those very, very tall, round-shouldered guys -- he was about six four -- with lousy teeth."

"The whole time he roomed next to me, I never even once saw him brush his teeth, They always looked mossy and awful, and he damn near made you sick if you saw him in the dining room with his mouth full of mashed potatoes and peas or something. Besides that he had a lot of pimples..."

Later, Holden argues with his roommate, Stradlater, who fails to appreciate a theme that Holden has written for him about Holden's deceased brother Allie's baseball glove. A womanizer, Stradlater has just returned from a date with Holden's old friend Jane Gallagher.

Holden asks Stradlater what he did with Jane:

"'What'd you do? Give her the time in Ed Banky's goddamn car?' My voice was shaking something awful.

'What a thing to say. Want me to wash your mouth out with soap?'

'Did you?'

'That's a professional secret, buddy.'"

The two roommates fight, Stradlater winning easily. Holden has had enough of Pencey Prep and catches a train to New York City where he plans to stay in a hotel until Wednesday, when his parents expect him to return home for Christmas vacation.

7) En route to New York, Holden meets the mother of a Pencey classmate and severely distorts the truth by telling her what a popular boy her "rat" son is:

"...Her son (Ernest Morrow) was doubtless the biggest bastard that ever went to Pencey, in the whole crumby history of the school. He was always going down the corridor, after he'd had a shower, snapping his soggy old wet towel at people's asses..."

Holden makes up lies to please Ernest's mother who comments:

"'Well. He's a very sensitive boy. He's really never been a terribly good mixer with other boys...'"

"Sensitive. That killed me. That guy Morrow was about as sensitive as a goddamn toilet seat."

Holden's Manhattan hotel room faces windows of another wing of the hotel, and he observes assorted behavior by "perverts." Holden struggles with his own sexuality.

He meets three women in their thirties, tourists from Seattle, in the hotel lounge and enjoys dancing with one but ends up with only the check.

Holden explains his pickup technique:

"I started giving the three witches at the next table the eye again. That is, the blonde one. The other two were strictly from hunger. I didn't do it crudely, though. I just gave all three of them this very cool glance and all. What they did, though, the three of them, when I did it, they started giggling like morons... 'Would any of you girls care to dance?' . .. Finally, the blonde one got up to dance with me..."

Holden started telling them lies to get their attention:

"'...I just saw Gary Cooper, the movie star, on the other side of the floor.'

'*Where*?' She asked me -- excited as hell. '*Where*?'"

Holden goes down to Greenwich Village and hangs out in Ernie's Nightclub:

"You could hardly check your coat, it was so crowded. It was pretty quiet, though, because Ernie was playing the piano. It was suppose to be something *holy*, for God's sake, when he sat down at the piano. Nobody's that good..."

"They were all shoving and standing on tiptoes to get a look at old Ernie while he played. He had a big damn mirror in front of the piano, with this big spotlight on him... You should've heard the crowd, though, when he was finished. You would have puked. They went mad. They were exactly the same morons that laugh like hyenas in the movies at stuff that isn't funny..."

While at Ernie's Nightclub a girl recognized Holden:

"...'Holden Caulfield!' Her name was Lillian Simmons. My brother D.B. used to go around with her for a while. She had very big knockers."

"'Hi,' I said... She had some Navy officer with her that looked like he had a poker up his ass."

"'How marvelous to see you!' Old Lillian Simmons said. Strictly a phony. 'How's your big brother?' That's all she really wanted to know."

Following a disappointing visit to Ernie's Nightclub, Holden agrees to have a prostitute, Sunny, visit his room. Holden has second thoughts, makes up an excuse, and pays the girl to leave. To his surprise, Maurice, her pimp, soon returns with her and beats up Holden for more money. He has lost two fights in one night. It is near dawn Sunday morning.

8) After a short sleep, Holden telephones Sally Hayes, a familiar date, and agrees to meet her that afternoon to go to a play:

"...'I was wondering if you were busy today. It's Sunday, but there's always one or two matinees going on Sunday... Would you care to go?'"

"'I'd love to. Grand.'"

"Grand. If there's one word I hate, it's grand. It's so phony..."

Meanwhile, Holden leaves the hotel, checks his luggage at Grand Central Station, and has a late breakfast. He meets two nuns, one an English teacher, with whom he discusses Romeo and Juliet.

Holden looks for a special record for his 10-year-old sister, Phoebe, called "Little Shirley Beans." He spots a small boy singing "If a body catch a body coming through the rye," which somehow makes Holden feel less depressed.

9) Sally is snobbish and "phony," but the two watch a play featuring married Broadway stars Alfred Lunt and Lynn Fontanne. Sally and Holden skate at Radio City but fight when Holden tries to discuss things that really matter to him and suddenly suggests that they run off together.

Holden leaves, sees the Christmas show at Radio City Music Hall, endures a movie, and gets very drunk. Throughout the novel, Holden has been worried about the ducks in the lagoon at Central Park. He tries to find them but only manages to break Phoebe's recording in the process. Exhausted physically and mentally, he heads home to see his sister.

10) Holden and Phoebe are close friends as well as siblings. He tells her that the one thing he'd like to be is "the catcher in the rye." He would stand near the edge of a cliff, by a field of rye, and catch any of the playing children who, in their abandon, come close to falling off.

When his parents return from a late night out, Holden, undetected, leaves the apartment and visits the home of Mr. Antolini, a favorite teacher, where he hopes to stay a few days. Startled, Holden awakes in the predawn hours to find Antolini patting Holden's head. He quickly leaves.

11) Monday morning, Holden arranges to meet Phoebe for lunch. He plans to say good-bye and head west where he hopes to live as a deaf-mute. She insists on leaving with

him, and he finally agrees to stay. Holden's story ends with Phoebe riding a carrousel in the rain as Holden watches.

12) In the final chapter, Holden is at the sanitarium in California. He doesn't want to tell us any more. In fact, the whole story has only made him miss people, even the jerks.

Holden Caulfield -- Why BPD?:

A number of assessments of Holden Caulfield's Borderline Personality Disorder symptoms have been available online or in publications. I'll attempt to combine some of them to present a more comprehensive analysis.

The Catcher in the Rye, by J.D. Salinger, is an excellent example of the reality in which goes through many adolescent minds. Holden Caulfield, the main character, suffers from a Borderline Personality Disorder (BPD). The story is mainly about his struggles through a hard time in his life.

Holden has been put through some rather traumatic incidents in his past, such as his brother Allie dying. Holden has had to put up with changing schools more often than most other kids. He's a very smart kid, although his grades do not accurately show it.

One of the typical characteristics of those with BPD is "functional failures" -- many people with BPD, like Holden, are unable to apply their abilities. They show potential for high achievement. However, their emotional instability and cognitive disturbances prevent them from reaching that potential.

Holden's mind, in a way, is trying to protect him from being harmed psychologically. However, the way it works is simply complicating matters. He's not aware of this hidden psychological process.

What Holden's mind is doing is hiding the harsher parts of reality from being put into focus. That is, it is selectively blocking his thought process from potentially psychologically damaging events or actions that take place around him.

The problem with this, however, is that Holden is not facing reality. Although it may seem like a good thing in the short term, it is impossible to hide from your past forever. Holden is confused about the situation. He doesn't know what is going on.

He thinks that he is a happy person. Holden does whatever he can to pretend he is. But the recessed memories of troubles in his past tend to sneak up on him. He doesn't realize how severe his problems are. Because of it he tends to break down and become depressed sometimes even for insignificant reasons.

Furthermore, Holden also has a fairly addictive personality. When he finds something he really likes, he finds it rather hard to let go. He abuses alcohol, he speaks extremely highly about his sister (compared to how he talks about most other people, that is), and he finds it difficult to change his old habits. All of these symptoms put together cause Holden to have several insecurities.

These insecurities cause his relationships with others to wax and wane, his self-image to waver, and his emotions to seem almost impossible to explain accurately. Holden is generally disturbed with the world around him. He acts on impulse to convey to others his antagonistic view of society.

Although he sometimes is correct, it often seems that he is trying to exacerbate involving people he doesn't like possibly in an attempt to compensate for his own shortcomings.

Holden's opinionated view of others is one of the main causes as to why he is either loved or hated -- sometimes both -- but not too much in between. When all tied together, these symptoms almost unquestionably characterize Holden Caulfield with Borderline Personality Disorder.

The irony is Holden is constantly trying to find people to talk to, but then he feels as though he needs to be alone. This is an example of affective instability due to a marked reactivity of mood. Yo-yo emotions characterize Holden. He's unstable in the way that he doesn't know whether he wants to be in a quiet place to think or if he wants to talk to someone.

Because of his relationship with Sally, Holden shows a pattern of unstable and intense interpersonal relationships characterized by alternating between extremes of idealization and devaluation. At first he doesn't really want to go through with his date.

Then later on he tells Sally he loves her and that he wants her to run away with him. This is definitely a drastic change of him not wanting her at all to him wanting her forever.

Holden appears to be an alcoholic-in-training -- he spends a lot of his money on drinks and other frivolous things during his time alone in New York City. He's also somewhat impulsive and reckless -- does more dangerous things, such as hiring a prostitute, getting beaten and robbed by her pimp, and walking forty one blocks back to his hotel at night.

Although it isn't recurrent, Holden did mention that he thought about attempting suicide. Someone who thinks and talks of suicide usually has problems that can be solved if they get help and deal with them properly.

Some of Holden's problems probably arise from the fact his parents seem to prefer his other siblings, including the deceased Allie over him. It may also be the reason his parents keep sending Holden to boarding schools out of town -- so they don't have to deal with him most of the time. This to a teenager like Holden would cause some sort of psychological damage if he deduced that this might be a motive for his parents sending him to prep schools out of town.

Although he does not blatantly state that there are times when he feels "empty" or "lonely", he often finds himself in places where there are many people with which he can talk to. Holden gets fired up quite easily and has trouble controlling his bouts of anger.

This can lead to dangerous situations if he cannot tame his emotions. Take his fight with Stradlater or the pimp for example. If he had gotten in a fight with a stronger, adult male in a bar let's say, he might have been seriously injured depending on the intent of the man he's fighting.

Summary of Holden Caulfield's General Symptoms:

1) Suicidal behavior/self-harm: One of the most serious symptoms of BPD, suicidal thoughts or behavior. One can never know if a suicide threat is serious or not. But

suicidal actions or comments should never be taken lightly. While Holden is alone in a New York hotel room he laid in bed and thought about his unfortunate feelings.

"What I really felt like was jumping out the window. I probably would've done it, too, if I'd been sure somebody'd cover me up as soon as I landed."

Although his reasoning as to why he didn't jump out the window may be strange, it at least shows that he is somewhat able to control his actions in these situations.

2) Self-destructive behavior: In order to fuel his desire for having a bullet lodged into his stomach, Holden decides to drink hard alcohol. He is both drinking away his health and his problems. Unfortunately, Holden has yet to realize that hiding from his problems behind alcohol will imminently cause greater problems than before.

"But I'm crazy. I swear to God I am. About halfway to the bathroom, I sort of started pretending I had a bullet in my guts... I was on the way to the bathroom to get a good shot of bourbon or something to steady my nerves and help me really go into action."

3) Dissociation -- feeling out of touch with reality: Holden frequently suffers from delusional thoughts which fill his mind with bizarre thoughts and are often hostile.

"I pictured myself coming out of the goddamn bathroom, dressed and all, with my automatic in my pocket, and staggering around a little bit... with this blood trickling out of the side of my mouth a little at a time... holding onto my guts, blood leaking all over the place."

These delusions possibly could be consequences of bad childhood memories or the ideas from a disturbed mind.

"I pulled the old peak of my hunting hat around to the front... that way, I couldn't see a goddamn thing... I think I'm going blind," I said in this very hoarse voice. "Mother darling, everything's getting so dark in here."

Although he claims to be just horsing around, these actions are not typical of the "average" adolescent. They have a high probability of stemming from a bad childhood memory.

"Mother darling, give me your hand. Why won't you give me your hand?"

4) Roller coaster emotions -- wide mood swings: People with BPD often endure wide mood swings -- yo-yo emotions, causing them to be horribly depressed one moment and wonderfully happy the next. Holden, in a way probably not understandable to anyone else other than himself, became depressed by the simple thought of someone who likes to go to movies.

This type of behavior is very characteristic of BPD in how insignificant, minor things can hinder his ability to be happy. Furthermore, shortly after being depressed as hell, Holden became rather happy after buying a record for his sister.

"I can understand somebody going to the movies because there's nothing else to do, but when somebody really wants to go, and even walks fast so as to get there quicker, then it depresses hell out of me... Boy, it made me so happy all of a sudden."

Also, Holden was very anxious to visit his old teacher, Mr. Spencer. After deciding to go visit him "I ran all the way to the main gate, and then I waited a second till I got my breath."

Upon arriving and talking to Mr. Spencer, however, Holden had a change of heart:

"All of a sudden then, I wanted to get the hell out of the room."

Emotions which wax and wane:

Holden's feelings for the significant people in his life change rapidly and drastically. After leaving the bar he was at, Holden was on his way to call his good friend Jane. However, by the time he had reached the telephone booth his mood had changed and he decided not to call Jane up at all.

"Finally what I felt like, I felt like giving old Jane a buzz and see if she was home yet. So I paid my check and all. Then I left the bar and went out where the telephones were. But when I got inside this phone booth, I wasn't in the mood any more to give old Jane a buzz."

5) Intense but short episodes of anxiety: Holden's brother, D.B., took Phoebe and him to see Hamlet. Holden was very excited about the idea of seeing the play. However, after actually seeing it he was no longer as enthralled about it as he previously was: "I was anxious as hell to see it, too. But I didn't enjoy it much."

Holden goes into great length about how anxious he was to see his old friend Jane because she was in the building. After sharing numerous stories about the fun things Jane and him used to do together to his roommate, he decided that he wasn't actually in the mood and didn't go to see her.

"'Jane Gallagher. Jesus.' I couldn't get her off my mind. I really couldn't. 'I oughta go down and say hello to her, at least.'

'Why the hell *don'tcha*, instead of keep saying it?' Stradlater said.

I walked over to the window, but you couldn't see out of it, it was so steamy from all the heat in the can. 'I'm not in the mood right now,' I said. I wasn't, either. You have to be in the mood for those things."

6) Emptiness: Many people with BPD report feeling painfully empty inside. They have cravings for something more, but they can't identify what that something more is. Out of the various symptoms of BPD, chronic feelings of emptiness can be the most psychologically damaging.

Holden says, "It made you depressed, and every once in a while, for no reason, you got goose flesh while you walked. It didn't seem like Christmas was coming soon. It didn't seem like anything was coming."

Feeling empty inside can play mind games in your head, causing simple desires to become cravings which seem infinitely impossible to obtain. These thoughts, which consume Holden's mind at times, make it so he is unable to appreciate the positive things in life.

"I don't get hardly anything out of anything. I'm in bad shape. I'm in lousy shape," Holden says.

7) Worries about abandonment: Holden has a rather addictive personality. When he finds something he likes a lot it is hard for him to let go. While talking to Sally in a bar after skating with her, Holden tells about his feelings for her:

"'You know something?' I said. 'You're probably the only reason I'm in New York right now, or anywhere. If you weren't around, I'd be someplace way the hell off. In the woods or some goddamn place. You're the only reason I'm around, practically.'"

Holden feels as though Sally is his only reason for living. He is scared of what would happen to him if something happened to her because she means his entire life to him. Holden is also afraid of leaving the place where he has spent most of his time at recently.

After getting kicked out of one of his schools, Holden won't leave until he is about to admit to himself that he is in fact no longer able to stay.

"What I was really hanging around for, I was trying to feel some kind of good-by. I mean I've left schools and places I didn't even know I was leaving them. I hate that. I don't care if it is a sad good-by or a bad good-by, but when you leave a place I like to know I'm leaving it. If you don't, you feel even worse."

8) Up-and-down pattern of unstable relationships: Relationships involving people with BPD resemble revolving doors. People with BPD often see other people as either all good or all bad, and these judgments can flip from day to day or even from hour to hour.

The most distinguishing symptom of BPD is that of a love-hate relationship with others. Holden talks with Sally about his plans of him marrying later in life.

"Then, when the dough runs out, I could get a job somewhere and we could live somewhere with a brook and all and, later on, we could get married or something... Honest to God, we could have a terrific time!"

However, shortly after expressing his love for Sally, Holden's ideologies turned a steep corner towards the opposite direction.

"'I was beginning to hate her, in a way... No, there wouldn't be. There wouldn't be oodles of places to go at all. I'd be entirely different,' I said. I was getting depressed as hell again."

9) Sensation seeking, impulsivity -- difficulty controlling emotions or impulses:

To count as a sign of BPD, this sensation-seeking symptom has to involve a minimum of two types of impulsive, self-destructive behaviors. These impulsive behaviors trigger adrenaline rushes and intense excitement.

Drug abuse: Holden has more than a few problems in his life, as most anyone should be able to figure out for themselves. To add to that, Holden has personally created more problems for himself in the addiction he has for alcohol.

"Boy, I sat at that goddamn bar till around one o'clock or so, getting drunk as a bastard. I could hardly see straight."

Holden has left the school and is in the big city all by himself. He is in need of a companion to save him from his lonesomeness and thus turned to his old friend Scotch.

Holden has a hard time expressing the emotions he keeps bundled up inside. When he does let out what he really is thinking, the way in which he expresses himself typically isn't well thought through.

"'C'mon, let's get outa here,' I said. 'You give me a royal pain in the ass, if you want to know the truth... I know I shouldn't have said it, and I probably wouldn't've ordinarily, but she was depressing the hell out of me.'"

Holden's troubles in how he explains his feelings are apparent when he talks about his dead brother.

"I just wish he wasn't there. You didn't know him. If you'd known him, you'd know what I mean. It's not too bad when the sun's out, but the sun only comes out when if feels like coming out."

Holden himself can't control his mind from wandering to negative thoughts about how others feel about him.

"I started thinking how old Phoebe would feel if I got pneumonia and died. It was a childish way to think, but I couldn't stop myself. She'd feel pretty bad if something like that happened."

Risky behavior: Holden, frustrated with society and how he fits in, doesn't really care too much for the consequences of his actions. That is, assuming he isn't so naive as to not understand what could happen to him if he does get caught by someone with authority over him.

Despite his fears that his parents would catch him and get him in trouble, Holden decided to visit his sister Phoebe in the middle of the night anyhow.

"I was afraid my parents might hear me sneaking in. But I decided I'd try it anyhow."

Holden got hustled by a hooker and a pimp at a New York City hotel for more money. He resisted and the pimp beat him.

"Then he smacked me. I didn't even try to get out of the way or duck or anything. All I felt was this terrific punch in my stomach."

It was risky behavior for Holden to get involved with street criminals like hookers and pimps.

10) Intense but short episode of depression: Holden tends to get depressed over seemingly insignificant events.

"...Then old Haas would just shake hands with them and then he'd go talk, for maybe a half an hour, with somebody else's parents. I can't stand that stuff. It drives me crazy. It makes me so depressed I go crazy. I hate that goddamn Elkton Hills."

Not only are the events that depress Holden insignificant, but the reaction he receives from them are severe yet usually short lived.

"When I finally got down off the radiator and went out to the hat-check room, I was crying and all. I don't know why, but I was. I guess it was because I was feeling so damned depressed and lonesome."

In both these instances Holden is teetered on the edge of losing it, but manages to either claim that he is alright or start hitting on waitresses within minutes after being in tears.

11) Thoughts of death: As Holden's mind wanders, as it commonly does, he somewhat often brings up thoughts of what it would be like when he was dead. These thoughts, which imply a desire of death, are disturbing and rather characteristic of people with BPD.

"I thought probably I'd get pneumonia and die. I started picturing millions of jerks coming to my funeral and all... I hope to hell when I do die somebody has sense enough to just dump me in the river or something."

12) Explosiveness -- inappropriate anger: Holden is often on the bring of becoming depressed due to his mental instability and insecurities. When even insignificant things bother him, he tends to lash out a retort on impulse, causing him to further alienate himself from society and give him more anger.

"Grand. There's a word I really hate. It's a phony. I could puke every time I hear it."

"That's something that drives me crazy. When people say something twice that way, after you admit it the first time."

Both of the above are examples of Holden inappropriately becoming angered. Even when significant things in his life are happening, like visiting his dead brother's grave, he irrationally feels insulted by the other people at the cemetery because they have things which Allie doesn't.

"That's what really drove me crazy. All the visitors could get in their cars and turn on their radios and all and then go someplace nice for dinner -- everybody except Allie. I couldn't stand it. I know it's only his body and all that's in the cemetery, and his soul's in Heaven and all that crap, but I couldn't stand it anyway."

13) Unclear and unstable self-image: This symptom describes a failure to find a stable, clear sense of identity. People who exhibit this symptom may view themselves quite favorably at times, yet, at other times, they exude self-disdain.

As a result of other symptoms, it is incredibly hard for Holden to figure out who exactly he is. His insecurities cause him to, at some times, think rather highly of himself, while at others to aspire for death. Holden is starting to figure some of these problems out, but he's unaware of most of them.

"Oh, I have a few qualms, all right. Sure... but not too many. Not yet, anyway. I guess it hasn't really hit me yet. All I'm doing right now is thinking about going home Wednesday. I'm a moron."

Holden believes he is simply just going through a phase. Although this may be partially true, there are longer lasting problems that have and will continue to affect him unless treatment proves successful.

"'Look, sir. Don't worry about me,' I said. 'I mean it. I'll be all right. I'm just going through a phase right now. Everybody goes through phases and all, don't they?'"

Holden and BPD Criteria:

Holden Caulfield has shown a pervasive pattern of instability of interpersonal relationships, self-image and affects, and marked impulsivity beginning by early adulthood and present in a variety of contexts, as indicated by five or more of the following DSM list of nine symptoms -- and I count all nine symptoms applying to Holden:

1) Frantic efforts to avoid real or imagined abandonment

2) Pattern of unstable and intense interpersonal relationships characterized by alternating between extremes of idealization and devaluation

3) Identity disturbance -- markedly and persistently unstable self-image or sense of self

4) Impulsivity in at least two areas that are potentially self-damaging (substance abuse, reckless behavior)

5) Recurrent suicidal behavior, gestures, or threats, or self-mutilation behavior (thoughts about jumping from a hotel window)

6) Affective instability due to a markedly reactivity of mood

7) Chronic feelings of emptiness

8) Inappropriate, intense anger or difficulty controlling anger

9) Transient, stress-related paranoid ideation or severe dissociative symptoms.

CHAPTER 15: "TOM CAPANO, DEADLY SEDUCER" & BPD

On June 27, 1996, in the evening, Ann Marie Fahey, secretary to the governor of Delaware, vanished without a trace following a restaurant rendezvous with her secret lover of more than two years: Thomas Capano. One of Wilmington's most prominent and respected figures, a millionaire attorney and former state prosecutor, "Tommy" was a charming, soft-spoken family man.

But in the weeks and months that followed Fahey's disappearance, investigators would gradually uncover the shocking truth: Capano was a steely manipulator ,driven by power and greed -- and capable of brutal murder.

In a riveting narrative expertly documented by probing interviews, diary entries, and email correspondence, and with superb insight into the twisted motivations of a killer, Ann Rule chronicles a real-life drama of Shakespearean proportions: ambitions fall, love turns to obsession, family names are tainted, the facade of success crumbles -- and a beautiful but vulnerable young woman pays the ultimate price in a convoluted and deadly relationship.

Thomas Capano appeared to fit a diagnosis of BPD -- borderline personality disorder with some secondary APD (antisocial personality disorder) overlapping the BPD. The BPD diagnostic category often overlaps with other personality disorders, especially affective disorders; narcissistic, antisocial, histrionic, schizotypal personality disorders; and post-traumatic-stress disorder.

The official psychiatric term for a psychopath is antisocial personality disorder (APD). Thomas Capano was convicted of murdering Anne Marie Fahey.

Capano's BPD Symptoms:

1) Frantic efforts to avoid real or imagined abandonment: When Anne Marie Fahey tried to reject Capano, he decided to kill her instead of letter her go. As the judge at his murder trial said:

"No one except the defendant will ever know exactly how or why Anne Marie Fahey died. What is certain is that it was not a crime of passion but, rather, a crime of control. By all accounts, she had ceased to be the defendant's lover but had never escaped his sphere of influence, control, and manipulation. Anne Marie Fahey could not be permitted to end the relationship unless he said so. She could not be allowed to reject him."

2) Pattern of unstable and intense interpersonal relationships characterized by alternating between extremes of idealization and devaluation: Capano had a wife and two mistresses simultaneously. He used them, manipulated them, and murdered one in a rage.

3) Impulsivity in two or more areas that are potentially self-destructive: Capano was sexually acting-out and reckless in finally murdering one mistress.

4) Affective instability due to markedly reactivity of mood: Capano's intense anxiety, at times, drove him to control and kill.

5) Chronic feelings of emptiness: Capano tried to fill the black hole inside himself with sex from at least three different women.

6) Inappropriate anger: Capano took the stand and lashed out at the prosecutor when questioned. His rage gave him away to the jury.

CHAPTER 16: AILEEN WUORNOS, FEMALE SERIAL KILLER & BPD

In *Lethal Intent* by Sue Russell it is revealed that Aileen Wuornos had been diagnosed with Borderline Personality Disorder:

"What would be diagnosed as Lee's (Aileen Wuornos) Borderline Personality Disorder manifests itself with her 'splitting' behavior, her way of seeing things and people as black and white but never gray. As good or bad, but never a truly human mixture of both."

In January, 1991, pawnshop records led to the arrest of Aileen Carol Wuornos, 34, aka "Lee," an abusive, alcoholic manhater with a murderous hairtrigger temper. Wuornos began prostituting herself at age 12 for cigarettes and beer. At 15 she bore an illegitimate child, at 16 she took to the highways as a hitchhiking hooker.

In 1986, with a lengthy rap sheet and prison term under her belt, she entered into a relationship with Tyria Moore, 24. Tired of turning $20 tricks, Wuornos decided to rob her customers of everything they had -- including their lives.

There seem to be virtually no records of single female sexual serial killers operating in the way male serial killers do. The case of Aileen Wuornos, often cited as an example of a male-type female serial killer, seems to lack the sexual pathology of a male sexual killer.

Wuornos was a thirty-five-year-old Florida roadside prostitute who was convicted for shooting six men. Although she robbed her dead victims, her motive appears to have been revenge or rage induced as a result of a lifetime of real and perceived abuse.

Throughout the period of the murders, numerous other lesser charges were laid against her under different aliases for threatening people with a weapon, assault, vandalism of her apartment, and other minor offenses.

She constantly traveled with a loaded handgun. In one town she was charged with making threatening calls to a supermarket chain over a lottery ticket dispute, and in another with assaulting a bus driver over a fare dispute. Addicted to cocaine and possibly crystal meth, she was wired up into a highly aggressive state of rage.

Her victims were elderly male motorists. Either they mistook her for a woman needing assistance or a hitchhiker, or they picked up Wuornos for sex.

Their bodies were found dumped in remote areas, often shot several times in the back of the head, and their pockets turned inside out or their clothes stolen in their entirety.

Their vehicles were found elsewhere, with property removed from them. There was no evidence, however, of torture or mutilation of the victims.

At her trial Wuornos claimed that she shot these victims in self-defense when they attempted to rape and assault her during her encounters with them.

Indeed, it turned out that her first victim, Richard Mallory, had served ten years for a violent rape. The other five victims, however, had no records of sexual assaults. The likely scenario is that Wuornos shot Mallory in self-defense and found herself afterward in a raging addiction to kill more.

Perhaps some real or imagined slight during her encounters with her elderly victims triggered her murderous acts. Maybe they reminded her of her grandfather, who abused her and who she thought was actually her father until age thirteen.

Wuornos was raped at age fourteen and gave birth to a son, who was given up for adoption. She led a life of prostitution and drug addiction and claimed she was raped five more times before age eighteen.

During her trial Wuornos became a cause for some factions of the feminist movement, who believed that her crimes were a response to systematic abuse at the hands of men.

Whether or not Wuornos is to be believed -- and certainly her claims are plausible -- her childhood and adolescent history is comparable to that of many male serial killers who did not get a break from the justice system. Neither did Wuornos: She was executed in Florida on October 9, 2002.

Wuornos is often presented as a sexual killer because the offenses took place in the context of her prostitution. But it is highly debatable whether her killings gave Wuornos any sexual gratification in the way male sexual serial killers derive theirs.

Wuornos & BPD symptoms:

She seems to have had five or more of the nine symptoms for a diagnosis of Borderline Personality Disorder:

1) Sensation seeking, impulsivity: Wuornos did a lot of sexual acting-out, substance abuse (alcohol and drugs), reckless behavior.

2) Roller coaster emotions: Besides anxiety and stress from childhood abuse and rapes, a slight or sign of disrespect from her hooker customers could result in rage and murder.

3) Explosiveness: Wuornos ended up in legal entanglements as a result of her rages.

4) Worries about abandonment: Wuornos felt abandoned by her parents and family.

5) Unclear and unstable self-concept: Wuornos viewed herself with self-disdain because of the rough lifestyle she led and an abused childhood. Her sexual identity varied -- she initially had sex with men and continued to in prostitution. But she got involved with a woman romantically.

6) Emptiness: Wuornos tried to fill her emptiness by killing her tricks and robbing them.

7) Up-and-down relationships: Wuornos relationships were like a revolving door. She saw people as all good or all bad, then her judgments flipped from day to day or even from hour to hour.

CHAPTER 17: WHO GETS BPD AND WHY?

There are three factors to be considered:

1) The contributions of childhood challenges

2) The influences of culture on personality

2) Uncovering the biological and genetic factors behind BPD

Childhood & Increased Risk of BPD:

Children can be quite resilient. Many children who have experienced difficult parents, early separation and loss, and even abuse and trauma manage to lead emotionally healthy lives.

In addition to a negative childhood experience, a genetic or biological predisposition can add to the risk of Borderline Personality Disorder. And cultural factors can contribute to BPD.

But extreme and persistent forms of childhood problems can be a partial cause of BPD.

Parenting styles -- problematic parenting:

Current professional and research perspectives on parenting and its true long-terms effects to partly cause BPD remain murky. So any theory on BPD development should be open to discounting a particular factor or set of influences.

--Emotional invalidation:

Marsha Linehan promotes the idea that "emotional invalidation" plays a critical role in BPD development. *Emotional invalidation* is a theory that refers to a variety of ways parents may diminish, demean, discount, and disqualify children's emotional experiences. Here are ten examples of the wrong thing parents say their children:

1. You shouldn't feel that way.

2. What are you crying about?

3. You're exaggerating.

4. That's just not true!

5. You're just like your father (brother, uncle, aunt, whomever).

6. I sure wish you could be more like your sister (cousin, father, aunt, or whomever).

7. Grow up!

8. Tell me something good that's happened.

9. You're being selfish.

10. You're way too young to try something like that. You could (get hurt, get in trouble, get lost, or whatever). Always ask me first before you do anyting!

"Emotional invalidation" as a BPD factor:

It's possible parents using "emotional invalidation" comments with their children can create negative factors contributing to BPD. Children could feel their identity discounted, passively withdraw, or get in the habit of over-reacting with extreme emotions and behaviors to get attention.

Also, it is possible sexual abuse could be covered up indirectly if the parent is in denial and uses "emotional invalidation" remarks to squelch or suppress bad news.

Dangers of "emotional invalidation" theory:

A) First, it is easy to send parents on a guilt-trip when they know their kids best. The meaning of what a parent says depends on the parent-child relationship. A parent could end up spoiling or negatively enabling children by obsessively avoiding "emotional invalidation" responses.

B) For example, if a parent always "validates" and reinforces what a child says or complains about to make the child always feel good, the parent could promote a sense of entitlement in the child.

C) Then as the child grows up they are stuck with an immature sense of entitlement -- they can't tolerate frustration, delay gratification, or recover from adversity. The unintended outcome is that the parent helps the child develop into a "movie-star" mentality or spoiled narcissist. They've learned to manipulate people by trying to send them on a guilt-trip -- adult spoiled-brat could result.

--Dysfunctional and disorganized families:

The dysfunctional family label has become somewhat of a cliché since everybody can point to some conflicts in their families. The point is that families where dysfuction and disorganization dominate create problems for their children and parents.

Fights, unresolved conflicts:

Dysfunction occurs when parents fight, express marital discord such as in loud arguments. If parents try to hide conflicts from the kids, the children pick up on subtle signs of tension when problems are not resolved.

Family role confusion:

Some parents retreat from parenting and put the burden of parenting on their oldest children. An older child may be pressured to accept excessive responsibility by a weak parent. Or a parent may treat their child as incompetent -- infantilizing them as if they're a baby forever.

Disorganized chaos -- unmanageable families:

Chaotic atmospheres interfere with a child's emotional development. Here are eight examples of disorganized chaos in dysfunctional family homes:

1) Financial woes, unpaid bills, and bill collectors

2) Frequent job changes

3) Constant moves from one neighborhood or city to another

4) Conflicts that cause various family or household members to move in and out

5) Substance abuse (alcohol, drugs)

6) Incarceration (parent or guardian is in jail or prison)

7) Neighborhood crime, dangerous street people

8) Disability, serious illness, or severe emotional disorders in one or more of the parents

Abuse and Trauma:

Abuse and trauma seems to raise the risk of developing BPD. Childhood abuse inflicted by parents, a relative, a bully, or a stranger is often reported by those diagnosed with BPD.

Research reveals that BPD can develop without trauma so that it is a separate category from PTSD (Post-Traumatic Stress Disorder). Other factors such as chaotic childhoods, emotionally invalidating experiences, and biological predispositions can lead to BPD in some cases.

Some people experience abuse and trauma but don't develop BPD or PTSD. Some are resilient because of personality strengths, genetic makeup, family support or psychotherapy.

However, abuse and trauma delivered by a family member usually has greater impact than trauma inflicted by a stranger. Long-term sexual molestation and incest is more likely to be one of the causes of BPD than a single attack by a stranger.

Yet, in the absence of genetic vulnerability or other risk factors, many children eventually manage to overcome some of the damaging effects of abuse and trauma.

Memory researchers such as Elizabeth Loftus have revealed that some therapists, who assume everyone with BPD or other mental disorders were victimized by childhood abuse and trauma hidden in their unconscious mind, often guide people to construct memories of events that evidence later shows never occurred.

The Influences of Culture on Personality:

The influence of cultural factors varies across cultures. The focus here is on the American culture. Five possible cultural influences on BPD are:

1) Individualism

2) Adolescence

3) Entitlement

4) Family instability

5) Technology

Individualism -- emphasis on me versus we:

The cultural theory is that because the American culture via parents, teachers, and role models encourages individual achievement on your own, individualism leads to a me focus. In more traditional cultures, such as those in the Far East, the community, family, and interdependence is emphasized.

The theory is that self-absorption increases the risk of a range of physical and emotional problems, including:

1) Eating disorders

2) Anger

3) Alcoholism

4) Drug abuse

5) Self-harm

6) Depression

7) Anxiety

8) Sensation seeking

This is not to blame people with BPD as being too self-absorbed or self-centered. This cultural theory is just one possible factor in many.

Adolescence and BPD:

Cultural theorists point to the modern American adolescent as having too much time on their hands -- time to get into trouble. When kids were busy on a farm milking cows and gathering crops, they had much less time for adolescent angst.

Teenagers with a lot of time sometimes get into trouble in gangs, violence, substance abuse (drugs, alcohol), sensation seeking, eating disorders, and risky sexual behavior. Adolescence is not a cause of BPD.

But it seems to be a factor in contributing a vulnerable time when BPD type symptoms can emerge.

Entitlement -- feeling too good:

A modern, industrial society, like the U.S.A., via the media, advertising, and peer pressure promotes feeling and looking good at all costs. Suffering is out.

Today, people look to pills, drugs, alcohol to solve every little emotional distress. Ads sell products to fix wrinkles, splotches, tiny imperfections as if they're major diseases. Everything from cars to fashion items are sold to make one happy, sexually attractive, and successful.

Hollywood movies, the media, advertising sells us on feeling good at all times -- we are entitled to have all our needs met instantly. When people are frustrated and things don't go their way they may freak out.

But the hallmark of a healthy personality is the ability to tolerate frustrations, delay gratification, and recover from adversity. So this entitlement aim of the culture can produce some BPD type symptoms in theory.

Family instability:

In the last sixty years, divorce, single-parent families, and unmarried parents are much more common. If people marry it is later in life. Large extended families are less common. Immediate families (Mom, Dad, two kids, for example) may be spread out across the world.

As a result, sources of emotional support are much less reliable and stable than they once were. Family instability may not be a direct cause of BPD but social support protects people against declining mental and physical health.

Technology and its isolating effects:

Technology can prevent the in-person contact you need to build relationships and trust. To get better, people with BPD need real relationships, real social support, and real feedback about their behavior.

Today technology in the form of computers, cellphones, and the Internet have increased productivity, access to information, and the ability to communicate. People spend a lot of time isolated in a virtual, digital world socializing online such as via Facebook, Twitter, or the next new website.

Young people particularly get wrapped up in new technology including video games. For instance, the following leads to social isolation:

--Participating in live Webcasts rather than meeting up with friends at a local coffee shop

--Posting comments on discussion boards or in chat rooms instead of communicating face-to-face in social situations

--Conversing via emails and text messages rather than phone conversations

--Cybersnooping friends' profiles rather than getting to know them personally

--Joining a World of Warcraft team rather than a soccer team

Again, no one theory fully accounts for BPD but isolating via technology could be a factor in some individuals' BPD development.

Genetics and Biology -- BPD in the Family Tree:

The nature-nurture issue with respect to BPD is complex. BPD sometimes is more common in some families. It could be a genetic tendency or it could be the result of people living together in a dysfunctional family or a combination of both.

Studying twins to find genetic causes:

A few twin studies comparing the incidence of BPD in identical vs. fraternal twins have been done. Some researchers claim 40 to 60% of BPD can be predicted by genetic factors. It may be that some genetic predispositions to BPD may lead to:

1) Impulsivity, sensation seeking

2) Unstable, highly reactive emotions

These symptoms are not sufficient to develop BPD. But combine impulsivity, sensation seeking and unstable emotions with other risks factors such as problematic or abusive parenting and cultural influences and one could be on the fast track to BPD development.

Possible twin studies weakness:

Dr. Leon Festinger, a professor of psychology at The New School for Social Research, Graduate Faculty, pointed out to me that genetic factors may have nothing to do with twins breaking down with Borderline Personality Disorder or other mental disorders.

Dr. Festinger (*Theory of Cognitive Dissonance*) honored me by admitting me to his small graduate seminar at The New School where I received my Ph.D. in psychology.

Dr. Festinger's insight was that identical twins could develop the same mental disorder, such as Borderline Personality Disorder, because of narcissism. The twins look alike and copy or emulate each other out of a narcissistic phenomenon. Researchers sometimes make assumptions about genetic theories when a counter-intuitive explanation is possible.

Dr. Elizabeth Loftus, another psychology professor of mine from the Graduate Faculty, The New School for Social Research, who instructed me while I was completing my Ph.D. in psychology, made an excellent observation about neurophysiology studies:

"Studying neurophysiology to reveal the psychology of personality or memory is like studying the grooves in a record to tell the difference between jazz and rock music."

On the other hand, smart genetic research can be done -- Dr. Sarnoff Mednick, another one of my grad school psychology professors at The New School for Social Research, was doing longitudinal genetic research in clinical psychology. I visited his research office in Denmark.

Dr. Mednick was using folk registers which are common in Scandinavian countries. They keep track of mental hospital admissions, prison admissions, and other health-related statistics in the folk registers which are systematic sources going back many generations.

Dr. Mednick found that he could predict who would break down with schizophrenia and other mental disorders by tracing medical histories of parents, grandparents, and earlier generations of the subjects in the study. He also did therapy interventions.

Biology and the BPD Equation:

Genetics can influence the likelihood of BPD symptoms such as impulsivity and roller-coaster emotions. Research has been done in these biological areas with respect to BPD:

1) Brain chemistry:

Nerve cells in the brain communicate through chemical messengers called neurotransmitters. Serotonin, one such neurotransmitter, seems to be particularly influential in BPD. Serotonin is involved in aggression, impulsivity, and mood stability.

Studies have shown that some people with BPD have disruptions in the way serotonin is used in the brain. However, medications that increase the availability of serotonin in the brain have not been as helpful in treating BPD as they have in treating other mental disorders. Thus, the exact role of serotonin in BPD remains unclear.

2) Brain structures:

The brain has numerous structures that process information, emotions, memories, and events. Recent studies have linked problems in the emotion-regulating circuits of the brain to BPD. The amygdala has been is one structure that has been studied with respect to BPD.

3) Brain functions:

Brain functioning refers to the tendency of certain brain areas to activate or inactivate under various conditions.

The problem with brain & neurophysiology studies:

A) What came first? The chicken or the egg? Do deficiencies in the brain chemistry, structure, and function come before or after BPD?

B) Studying neurophysiology and making assumptions about psychology including BPD is like Dr. Loftus said, "Like studying the grooves of a record to determine the difference between jazz and rock & roll music."

CHAPTER 18: MYTHS ABOUT BPD

Some of the myths about Borderline Personality Disorder include the assumption that BPD people are always malicious, crazy, irrational, violent, and disregard others. BPD results from individuals attempting to meet basic human needs -- although sometimes misguided.

Here are some common myths:

A) BPD people are manipulative, attention seeking

B) BPD diagnosed individuals are violent, at high risk for harming others

C) One has BPD for life

D) There is no treatment for BPD

E) Bad parenting causes BPD

F) BPD sufferers are crazy, irrational

G) Only women have BPD

Myth A -- BPD people are manipulative & attention seeking

Because BPD sometimes involves self-harm or suicidal behavior, people respond quickly to help. Helpers can feel fear, anger, sadness, guilt, and confusion. So it seems on the surface that BPD people are using suicidal or self-injury behavior to manipulate and get attention.

Because a suicide attempt results in help and attention for the BPD suicidal person, doesn't mean they are intending self-harm to manipulate and get attention. The BPD person is not manipulative -- they're just desperately trying to fill a need or get help.

Myth B -- BPD people are violent or at high risk for harming others

People with BPD are generally not violent and at low risk for harming others. They tend to sacrifice their own needs to keep others happy so they won't reject or leave them. They fear abandonment.

The cases discussed in earlier chapters regarding characters in Hollywood movies or in literature are very exceptional cases where murder was involved. Those murdering characters were included to illustrate BPD in a dramatic, entertaining way.

In most BPD people anger is turned inward. They may avoid expressing anger or aggression because of negative experiences they've had themselves -- such as childhood abuse or trauma.

C) BPD is a lifetime sentence

Particularly years ago people sometimes considered BPD incurable. Some clinicians might not diagnose a person with BPD because it might seem to them that BPD was untreatable. But there have been some advances in therapy and BPD has a good prognosis if treated with effective methods and medication if needed.

D) BPD is untreatable

In the past therapy was not too effective with BPD because it was not aimed at BPD. There is evidence now that some therapies (cognitive, behavioral, psychoanalytic, for example) can work with BPD.

Later in the book I introduce my own new therapy for BPD which I believe is more effective than any other therapy. I'll discuss more about it later.

E) Parenting problems cause BPD

It is a myth that BPD is caused simply by abusive parents, bad mothering in early childhood, or dysfunctional families. However, increased risk for BPD can result from neglect, abuse, and trauma delivered by dysfunctional parents. Most BPD people don't report a history of abuse, trauma, and neglect.

Stressful experiences and certain personality traits can lead to BPD. For instance, a person might not fit in well or get along with his family. He might be reserved while his family members are very emotional. Thus, one could feel excluded like a black sheep or a round peg not fitting into a square hole. This is an example of one possible stressor.

Perhaps the parents don't have the time needed by a sensitive and emotional child -- not because they're neglecting the child --because of their career or work schedules. A teenager might have experienced stress at school or from his/her peers which puts them at risk for BPD.

F) BPD people are psychotic, crazy, and irrational

People with BPD are in pain and, at times, say or do things they later regret. They have a lot of negative emotions they experience intensely.

On the positive side BPD people can experience excitement, joy, and happiness more intensely than the average person.

BPD people may have had experiences such as abuse, neglect, rejection. Therefore, if they react strongly to the possibility of being abandoned or rejected, it could be based on being burned in the past.

G) Only women have BPD

Because culturally women are more expected to be emotional, express feelings, and rely on relationships, it may be that some diagnostic tendencies reflect that. About three times as many woman are recognized as BPD types vs. men. Sometimes men are diagnosed as ASPD (antisocial personality disorder) when they fit BPD if the assessment was more objective.

CHAPTER 19: SENSATION SEEKING, IMPULSIVITY & SELF-HARM

TWO MAJOR BPD SYMPTOMS:

Potentially Dangerous Impulsive Behavior:

When one acts impulsively he's ignoring future negative outcomes and not thinking before acting. BPD people seek excitement and drama to fill the empty spiritual hole inside themselves. They may feel momentarily better in the present but then later feel guilty, anxious, and hate themselves.

A case could be made that bombing is an addiction to fill the existential, spiritual void within. For example, *The Weather Underground*, a documentary telling "The explosive story of America's most notorious revolutionaries", illustrates how alienated college students can get addicted to the danger of bombing.

For years, from the '60s to the '70s, young rebels in their teens and twenties committed terrorist bombings, rationalizing their thrill-seeking behavior under the cover of political activism. No doubt some of them were BPD people escaping their feelings in a misguided attempt to fill the empty spiritual hole inside themselves.

Bernardine Dohrn snarled, "Hello. I'm going to read a declaration of war... Within the next 14 days we will attack a symbol or institution of American injustice..."

Forty years ago, with these words, a group of young American radicals called The Weathermen announced their intention to overthrow the U.S. government. Fueled by outrage over the Vietnam War and racism in America, they went underground during the 1970s, bombing targets across the country that they felt symbolized "the real violence" that the U.S. government and capitalist power were wreaking throughout the world.

From pitched battles with police on Chicago's city streets, to bombing the U.S. Capitol building, to breaking acid-guru Timothy Leary out of prison, this carefully organized clandestine network attempted to incite a national revolution, while successfully evading one of the largest FBI manhunts in history.

While former Weathermen members claim that idealistic passion drove them, it would seem that the real reason for this thrill-seeking, reckless, terrorist behavior had more to do with their internal emptiness, boredom, and addiction to danger.

The Weathermen was sort of cultish, a group of kindergarten radicals -- "Join us or fuck you!" Because some of them had come from sheltered, upper-middle class homes, this was the most exciting thing of their lives -- a political excuse to raise hell, join in "the days of rage."

Some of the more routine sensation-seeking BPD people engage in, aside from radical bombers, include:

A) Spending: Impulsive spending means out-of-control buying binges. Shopaholics buy a lot of unnecessary stuff. The BPD person might buy 100 pairs of shoes or fill their closet up with clothing they don't need.

The twelve-step program DA -- Debtors Anonymous aims to help impulsive spenders and debtors. No matter how much the BPD impulsive spender buys, he/she can't fill the emotional void within.

B) Gambling: If someone can set a reasonable limit and gamble once in a while, it isn't a problem. But BPD people who are impulsive gamblers aim to get a rush out of gambling with out-of-control betting to fill the emptiness they feel within.

In extreme cases they may take out a second mortgage on their home, resort to forgery, embezzlement, and theft to raise money to continue gambling.

Gamblers Anonymous, a twelve-step program, was formed to help impulsive, problem gamblers recover.

In the movie, *The Cooler*, Bernie Lootz (William H. Macy), the unluckiest man in Vegas -- he's a "cooler." His bad luck is so contagious that Shelly Kaplow (Alec Baldwin), the last of the old-time mobsters, uses Bernie to kill the high rollers' action at his casino. But when Bernie meets Natalie (Maria Bello) and falls in love, he gives a whole new meaning to being "unlucky in love."

In the past, when Bernie's gambling addiction gets out of control, Shelly cripples Bernie by bashing, knee-capping him with a baseball bat. Bernie says he's grateful to Shelly for stopping his gambling addiction the hard way.

Robert DeNiro, Sharon Stone, and Joe Pesci star in *Casino*, a riveting look at how blind ambition, white-hot passion, and 24-karat gold toppled an empire. Las Vegas 1973 is the setting for this fact-based story about the Mob's multi-million dollar casino operation where fortunes and lives were made and lost with the roll of the dice.

When the Robert DeNiro character marries the hustler played by Sharon Stone, he's mixing too many addictions -- gambling, substance abuse, sex, and love. Toss the mobster character Joe Pesci into the mix and the result is self-destruction for all these characters.

C) Binge eating: Some BPD people do binge eating to try to feel better. They'll eat a big carton of ice cream, a whole box of cookies, a giant bag of salty snacks, or whatever in excess to fight emotional emptiness. Then they feel uncomfortable, sick, and may vomit.

Overeaters Anonymous is the twelve-step program that addresses people with eating disorders.

D) Shoplifting: People with BPD sometimes resort to shoplifting, stealing items they don't need and can afford just for excitement or fear to overcome the empty boredom they feel. The media exploded with stories about Winona Ryder and Lindsay Lohan who were charged with shoplifting.

E) Reckless driving: To add danger and excitement to offset the empty spiritual void inside, some BPD people get into impulsive, reckless driving.

Road rage, running stoplights, excessive speeding, weaving from lane-to-lane without signaling, hair-raising and illegal U-turns are examples of reckless driving.

F) Reckless sex: Sex Addicts Anonymous is an example of a twelve-step program for people into impulsive, reckless sex. BPD people may be into reckless sex to increase the excitement in what they perceive as their empty, boring lives.

They have sex with a string of partners to put them at high risk for sexually transmitted diseases, unwanted pregnancies, and sometimes career damage. They may impulsively get into sadomasochistic sex, group sex, partner swapping, swinger parties, or exhibitionism.

Some BPD men, in particular, may resort to a parade of prostitutes or pornography. When escalating sexual activities doesn't fill the spiritual hole inside them, they may increase the sexual obsession and ultimately get into legal problems.

The film *Sex, Lies, and Videotape*, while an erotic comedy on one level, reveals how reckless sex can destroy a marriage and damage a career.

With smoldering sensuality and biting humor, the surprising relationship between the three title subjects is revealed in *Sex, Lies, and Videotape*, the most-talked about sex comedy of 1989. James Spader played Graham, a long-lost college friend who drifts back into town and into the lives of John (Peter Gallagher), a self-involved philanderer, his angelic wife, Ann (Andie MacDowell), and her saucy sister, Cynthia (Laura San Giacomo).

One by one, each is drawn into the very "personal" project Graham is working on, leaving the relationships between them forever transformed.

Some candidates for BPD exist in the three films *Final Analysis*, *Body Heat*, and *The Last Seduction*. *The lead male characters in these movies all are manipulated by seductive, sexually exciting women.*

Psychiatrist Isaac Barr is a noted expert in his field -- and the perfect patsy in a devious scheme of murder and inheritance. And his fall could be straight down from atop a towering lighthouse. Richard Gere and Kim Basinger face off on a lighthouse catwalk in Final Analysis, a gripping update of the complex psychological thrillers of yesteryear.

The mood is sinister: Barr (Gere) breaches professional ethics by romancing the gorgeous sister of a troubled client (Uma Thurman). One black widow makes a mystery exciting. Two make this one irresistible.

William Hurt and Kathleen Turner strike sparks in Lawrence Kasdan's *Body Heat*, a sexy, haunting tale of desire and skullduggery that echoes 1940s film noirs but is charged with an energy and passion that could only flare in the '80s. The William Hurt character seems to be a Borderline Personality Disorder type.

The Last Seduction -- Bridget Gregory (Linda Fiorentino) seems to have it all: beauty, intelligence and a marriage to Clay, a potentially wealthy physician (Bill Pullman). But everything isn't enough for Bridget, who persuades her husband to make dirty deals on prescription drugs and then runs with the profit. Now incognito in a mid-American small town, Bridget draws a naive local, Mike Swale (Peter Berg), into a smoldering affair.

Passion, greed and revenge forge a desperate triangle between the three as Bridget draws her unknowing victims deeper into her web of deadly deceit. Both the Bill Pullman and Peter Berg characters could be diagnosed as BPD people. Clay is a gambling addict sucked into drug dealing. Sex lures Mike into a murder plot.

G) Substance abuse: BPD people, by abusing drugs and alcohol, aim to escape their out-of-control emotions or fill the endless emptiness they feel. By using alcohol, marijuana, cocaine, ecstasy, or many other mood-altering drugs, BPD individuals hope to fill-up their hollow, meaningless lives.

Substance abuse is particularly dangerous in that it can further trigger other reckless, sensation-seeking such as reckless driving, out-of-control gambling, reckless sex adventures, shoplifting, and other addictions taking them over the edge.

Alcoholics Anonymous, Narcotics Anonymous, Cocaine Anonymous, and Marijuana Anonymous are some of the twelve-step programs helping BPD people and other addicts/alcoholics to recover.

People with BPD, who don't get proper treatment, sometimes cut their lives short via substance abuse, car accidents, unhealthy lifestyles, overeating, or suicide.

An example of substance abuse is illustrated by the movie *Less Than Zero*. Robert Downey, Jr. portrays Julian, a Beverly Hills brat who has it all: looks, charm, smarts, a rich father -- and a nasty drug habit. His friend (Andrew McCarthy) and girlfriend (Jami Gertz) are trying to help but only enable Julian to get worse.

Julian's world is crumbling so fast, he might just take them with him. The result is a powerful and compelling story of three kids who started out with everything... and are about to wind up with *Less Than Zero*. In this 1987 film, Julian ends up dead from drugs. Julian seems a possible BPD case history.

Self-harming Behavior & BPD:

Seeking to escape one's feelings or get help by self-harming or suicide is one symptom of BPD people. Take a look at three films with suicidal characters: *Winter Kills*, *The Long Goodbye*, and *One Flew Over The Cuckoo's Nest*.

Which of the three suicidal characters might be BPD people?

Winter Kills is the story of Nick Kegan (Jeff Bridges), the son of world-famous tycoon Pa Kegan (John Huston) and half-brother of the late President Timothy Kegan, who was slain by a lone assassin 19 years earlier.

But when a long-rumored "second gunman" makes a secret deathbed confession, Nick begins to unravel a trail of suspects that includes a billionaire war-freak (Sterling Hayden), a murderous Mob boss (Ralph Meeker), a shady nightclub owner (Eli Wallach), a Cuban kingpin (Tomas Milian), an eccentric computer expert (Anthony Perkins) and a mysterious Washington madam (Elizabeth Taylor).

This black comedy ends with Pa Kegan committing suicide by jumping off a tall building in Manhattan. As he heads for the street below, Pa Kegan yells at Nick to move the family fortune off-shore to Brazil. Is Pa Kegan a BPD type character?

The Long Goodbye showcases Elliot Gould as a quirky, mischievous Phillip Marlowe in a send-up of Raymond Chandler's classic detective story.

Los Angeles private eye Phillip Marlowe faces the most bizarre case of his life, when a friend, Terry Lennox (Jim Bouton), who apparently commits suicide, turns into a double murder involving Eileen Wade (Nina Van Pallandt), a sexy blonde, a disturbed gangster and a suitcase full of drug money.

But as Marlowe stumbles toward the truth, he soon finds himself lost in a maze of sex and deceit -- only to discover that in L.A., if love is dangerous... friendship is murder.

The sexy blonde's husband, Roger Wade (Sterling Hayden), an alcoholic writer, commits suicide -- The Long Goodbye -- by walking into the ocean. Marlowe's friend, Terry Lennox, just faked the suicide to escape the cops and the Mob. Which character is a BPD type?

One Flew Over The Cuckoo's Nest presents a suicidal character in the Billy character played by Brad Dourif who is one of the mental patients. Nurse Ratched (Louise Fletcher) threatens to tell Billy's mother than he slept with a girl on the ward. Billy then slashes himself in a suicide attempt.

It seems Billy from *One Flew Over The Cuckoo's Nest* portrays a BPD character. Another BPD person would seem to be Roger Wade in *The Long Goodbye*. Take a look at the films yourself and see what you think.

Types of self-harming acts/hurting for help:

A) Cutting: People self-harming by cutting often cut their arms, legs, and abdomens. Some display their cuts and some hide them. Tools vary including razor blades, scissors, paper clips, staples, needles, knives, and broken glass. Sometimes they use their own fingernails. In the past some punk rockers have cut themselves as a stylish way to rebel against society's norms.

Sometimes there is a functional purpose. When I was a prison psychologist, for instance, one inmate was cutting his wrists to get out of work details. I spoke to him in the prison infirmary and he revealed he was avoiding the "hoe squad" which involved using inmates to do hard labor in farm fields.

B) Burning: Some of the burning techniques involve cigarettes, lighters, and matches. The typical burn is over a small area of the body. However, over time numerous scars may occur.

C) Blunt force trauma: Kaysen in *Girl, Interrupted* used blunt force trauma to harm herself by banging her wrists against wooden surfaces.

The usual blunt force self-harm method involves pounding fists against walls, punching oneself, banging one's head into something hard, and using a hammer or other tool to inflict pain on one's body. Blunt force trauma sometimes results in bruises, scars, wounds, and even broken bones.

D) Skin picking and hair pulling: These skin picking and hair pulling symptoms are sometimes related to obsessive-compulsive disorder. It includes picking at cuticles and scabs, pulling out hair, and pinching the skin until it bleeds.

E) Intentional accidents: Some BPD people harm themselves in what initially seems to be accidental ways. However, when investigated it is found they have avoided reasonable precautions. They have accidents at home or at work that could have been avoided by being more careful or by using safety equipment or clothing.

For example, they might fall off ladders because they set it up improperly on unsteady ground. Or burn themselves by recklessly rearranging burning logs in a fireplace or campfire.

F) Rare behaviors: Some very unusual self-harming acts have included swallowing sharp objects, friction burning, eyeball pushing, biting one's own body, inserting objects into bodily cavities, or ingesting harmful but not fatal chemicals.

It is estimated that 2 million people in the United States have committed self-harming behaviors. Sometimes only medical staff in hospital emergency rooms see the results of self-harming acts. Many of these people have BPD.

Why do BPD people harm themselves? Here are eight possible theories:

Theory 1) To get attention -- communicating to or influencing other people:

Some professional clinicians don't believe that this motivation plays a large role because many BPD people try to hide self-harm injuries from others.

If the BPD person lacks the skills to get support from others, sometimes they use self-harming behavior to elicit the concern they seek.

Some BPD people have a history of people invalidating their feelings or ignoring what they say. Thus, others have no idea how much pain they're in. Or the BPD person has not learned how to express their feelings to other people or share how they're feeling.

The BPD individual may have difficulty asserting himself or skillfully communicating what he wants. So he/she might resort to self-harm behavior or suicide attempts.

Theory 2) To distract from negative feelings -- relief or escape from emotional pain:

BPDs may use self-harming behavior to cope with unbearable inner or emotional pain. Physical pain distracts them from crushing internal emotional torment.

Research studies have shown most BPD people expected to get relief from their emotional distress by self-harm or attempting suicide. Although it seems counter-intuitive, many BPD people have reported in studies that they feel better emotionally after they've hurt themselves physically.

For many BPDs, it seems the short-term benefit of feeling better after harming oneself, outweighs the long-term downside of self-harm or suicide attempts.

Sometimes a critical incident or upsetting event occurs and confuses the BPD person. They can't figure out how things will ever get better. So suicide illogically seems a way to feel better. Some may decide to act on suicidal thoughts or ideation.

Theory 3) To feel better:

When one injures one's body, your brain releases natural pain killers called endorphins. These endorphins then may help one return to a less stressful emotional condition. Thus, ironically, physical pain can lead to a regulation and reduction in emotional pain.

Another way to obtain a rush of endorphins is to eat hot chili peppers. The endorphin rush can be understood even by those who have no emotional disorders.

Theory 4) To feel something other than numbness and emptiness:

Sometimes BPD people inflict pain, self-harm, or attempt suicide in order to feel something "real". They feel unreal and out of touch with their surroundings.

They may dissociate or check out of their environment. The experience of dissociation, numbness, and emptiness is stress-inducing and can, from the BPD's viewpoint, be addressed by self-harm activity.

Of course it is a lot less logical to commit suicide over aiming to feel something "real" since once one's dead he can't feel anything. So in a crazy way, self-harm makes more sense if one aims to "feel" something.

Theory 5) To punish themselves -- self-punishment:

If a BPD person believes he deserves punishment or abuse, self-harm is a way they may go to get a punishment result. If the BPD individual perceives they've committed wrongdoing or feel guilty over an incident, self-harm is an answer to get self-punishment.

One situation is that a BPD type feels angry, frustrated, keyed-up, and thus energized to take action. While self-harm has negative consequences, it is one solution to one's problems.

If the aim of a BPD person is punishment and suffering, then self-harm would seem more appealing than suicide. With suicide they'd escape from their problems and their life. So when would they have time to suffer and get punishment if they're dead?

The problem with self-punishment is while it seems in the short-term to make the BPD feel bad about a mistake, one feels lower self-esteem. Therefore, losing a job or getting rejected in a relationship, results in a shattered self-concept. So if the BPD person feels worse about himself, how is he going to get a positive outlook for later success in the next job or relationship?

The origin of this self-defeating cycle of behavior could be from a childhood in an emotionally invalidating environment. If one is brought up being overly-punished, dismissed, criticized for struggling with emotions, then one could be trapped in a pattern of self-punishment and self-harm. Unfortunately this is a negative circular dynamic and self-harm is not the exit from it.

Theory 6) To get back at someone:

If the BPD individual can't express anger in an appropriate way, he may hurt himself to make others feel guilty for something they said or did that was offensive.

I was working in a state mental hospital as a psychologist and one case I had, for example, was a middle-aged woman who was reacting to incest. Someone in her family had sexually molested her as a child.

The incidents got to her later in life, she tried self-harm, and ended up with a major depression in the mental institution. She turned the anger inward and was trying on some level to punish the family member who sexually assaulted her.

Theory 7) To reenact their own abuse:

Many BPD people report that they were abused as children. Children often believe they deserve the abuse they get. And as adults some continue the pattern of self-punishment and self-harm.

Theory 8) Reducing a burden on other people:

Some BPD people report that they get into self-harm or suicide attempts to reduce the burden on people around them. They assume people would be better off if they weren't around with all their problems and volatile emotions.

But actually if one commits suicide, the people around you are much worse off. When people harm themselves or kill themselves, the surviving family, friends, co-workers, and acquaintances are often devastated.

If a BPD type kills himself, it takes a long time for family and particularly children to recover. Further, children of a person who commits suicide are at greater risk of committing suicide themselves. So self-harm or suicide does not reduce the burden on family, children, and friends.

Suicide -- the Final Escape:

It is estimated that 10 percent of BPD people ultimately commit suicide. Suicidal acts are among the most dangerous and complex impulsive behaviors BPD people commit.

Is suicide a cry for help or a revenge attempt?

Oblivion or death may seem the only option to a BPD person who feels helpless, hopeless, and in great emotional pain when things don't seem to go their way.

If one feels wronged, abandoned, or hurt, a suicide attempt may seem like a way to get back at the culprit. The thought might be that the enemies will feel guilty and remorse after their death.

Who's at risk for suicide?

Predicting who will commit suicide is complicated. BPD people are at higher risk than others. If one is a substance abuser then the suicidal tendencies also go up. If one has experienced a suicide in one's family, the odds of suicide for that person increase.

For those BPDs who have tried suicide in the past, it is more likely they will eventually commit suicide. For BPDs the more likely suicide risk is when they're in their 30s according to research.

After the BPD person gets psychotherapy, treatment including medications if needed, for suicidal symptoms and behaviors, the risk of suicide is reduced.

When should one seek professional help to prevent suicide?

1) If one shows a sharp loss of interest in things he or she used to enjoy in life.

2) The BPD person talks about feeling utterly hopeless and helpless.

3) When one expresses the view that the world would be better off without him or her.

4) The BPD individual talks about committing suicide.

5) He or she calls people to say goodbye.

6) When the person puts personal affairs in order -- as if they're not going to be around anymore.

7) After a period or depression or sadness, the person exhibits unusual calm.

8) He/she starts giving away prized possessions away without cause.

9) The BPD individual has experienced a serious recent loss.

What's the significance of sensation-seeking, impulsivity and suicidal behavior for BPD diagnosis?

Most BPD people show some impulsive, sensation-seeking, addictive behaviors. But not all BPD exhibit impulsive behavior or suicidal tendencies. Sensation-seeking, self-harm, and suicide is common among BPD people.

However, some with bipolar disorder and mania show depressed or high symptoms. Others have very specific diagnoses such as kleptomania -- impulsive stealing -- which may be separate from BPD. Some may show only signs of pathological gambling or substance abuse and no other symptoms of BPD.

CHAPTER 20: EXPLOSIVE FEELINGS & MOODS

BPD SYMPTOM:

The BPD tendency to get angry or anxious over small stuff and experience negative feelings or despair when good things happen is called "emotional dysregulation."

Emotional dysregulation:

Unstable emotions, rapid mood changes, and difficulty managing emotions such as anger is termed "emotional dysregulation."

Identifiable emotions include:

Happiness, sadness, anger, fear, disgust, surprise.

Primitive emotions:

Some researchers note that emotions linked to bodily reactions are called "primitive emotions." For instance, fears of falling, loud noises, abandonment, and some predators such as snakes and spiders, elicit genetic-encoded, instinctual responses lead them to feel certain emotions.

"Primitive emotions" are preprogrammed to warn people of possible danger. People with BPD may have super-charged physical responses to fears and the result is overreactive emotions.

Body-reaction emotion theory:

One camp of emotion theorists claims that emotions are the result of bodily reactions only. On the other side of the issue are the "thoughtful emotion" theorists.

The "bodily-reaction emotion" theorists claim fear, anger, disgust, happiness, sadness originate from the following list of bodily responses:

A) Muscle tension

B) Increased heart rate

C) Increased blood pressure

D) Sweating

E) Smiling

F) Laughing

G) Gagging

H) Jumping

I) Pupils dilating or constricting

J) Salivating

K) Frowning

Responses of BPD people:

There has been mixed results from research aimed at showing BPD people overreact in terms of startle responses. Contradictory results has puzzled researchers who assume BPD people react with greater emotional intensity.

Explanations for this inconsistency include:

1) Dissociation: People with BPD sometimes dissociate or mentally remove themselves from stressful events. Dissociation may reduce their physical reactions and in turn their emotional response.

2) Design of studies: Experimental designs or the structure of the study to trigger emotion is not a valid measure of natural emotion-evoking events. BPD people may overreact physically and emotionally but studies have not replicated the essence of real world events.

3) BPD reporting: BPD people don't experience stronger bodily reactions and emotions -- they just report stronger emotions during studies.

Thoughtful-emotion theory:

Many theorists view emotions as a result of thoughts which is a cognitive-emotion theory. For example, somebody rudely bumps into you on a train or bus. You start to get angry. Then you look and see the person who bumped you is blind. You are no longer angry.

Studies show BPD people strongly view events as more negatively than others. Distorted thinking by BPD individuals can cause a lot of emotional turmoil by overreacting.

Those who can regulate their emotions effectively use logic and reasoning to reinterpret events in a less threatening way.

For example, a BPD woman gets overly jealous and suspicious when her boyfriend goes out of town on business. She assumes he will cheat on her with another women. Then she rejects him and ends the relationship. This BPD woman has a higher risk of unstable relationships because of this negative overreaction.

Alternatively, a non-BPD woman may be temporarily suspicious when her boyfriend is out of town on business. But she considers the overall relationship positives and dismisses her fears. She has a lower risk of unstable relationships.

Unstable emotions & moods:

BPD people may more strongly react, be more easily upset by things people say or do, than others. A minor critical look or comment can stress them out. Their emotions yo-yo like a roller coaster ride. Thus, a BPD person may be happy one minute, sad the next, and angry a moment later.

Problem controlling anger:

In BPD people, negative emotions like shame, sadness, guilt, and especially anger are harder to cope with than in others. BPD people can, at times, get carried away with irritation turning to intense anger which can become out-of-control rage. Sometimes this is followed by a temper tantrum, throwing objects, yelling, threatening or fighting.

BPD emotional style:

A person with a healthy personality has emotional ups and downs. But the emotions seem appropriate.

BPD people tend to experience negative emotions more often than healthy personality people. BPD individuals have more anxiety, sadness, anger, and jealousy. They have less happiness. Their emotions race to extremes in seconds and take longer to calm than others.

Difficulty recognizing and expressing emotions:

Many BPD people are not aware of their current emotional states. For instance, they might be shaking their fist and shouting and if asked be unaware they are angry. There is a disconnection between how they express their emotions and what they say they feel.

They can perceive negative emotions in others accurately. But they tend to project negative feelings in others when others have a neutral expression.

Negative emotions about negative emotions:

BPD people have more negative emotions -- anxiety, depression, jealousy, resentments, and rage. But they make a bad mood worse by feeling bad about feeling bad. Anxiety and anger makes them depressed. They feel guilty and despair because of their jealousy and rage. The cycle of misery is self-inflicted by getting depressed about being depressed.

CHAPTER 21: BPD IDENTITY PROBLEMS

In self-concept and identity dysregulation, a person has no clear or stable sense of who he or she is. There is an emptiness, no defined core of identity or where the BPD person is headed.

Let's take an example of a young guy, Jim, who enters a Seattle college. Jim is always changing his life. He starts out in his freshman year with a major in business management. In his sophomore year he suddenly decides instead to major in geology. He's into geology field trips.

By the end of his sophomore year he is turned off by geology and switches his major to drama and theater arts. Jim then drops out of college, travels to Los Angeles to be an actor. After an audition or two he can't take rejection.

Jim quits acting, takes a job as a waiter at a restaurant, and gets fired for angry outbursts against customers. He takes a job as a receptionist at a fitness gym.

He changes his religion from Baptist and joins a religious cult. He can't get along with the cult members and quits religion completely.

Jim changes his preppy style of dress to a punk style, gets some piercings, tattoos, and grungy clothing. He decides he wants to join a punk rock band but he can't play an instrument or sing.

He gets into drugs and alcohol, gets a DUI -- arrested for drunk driving, and ends up in a sober living center. Jim complains in group therapy that he has no idea who he is, feels empty inside, and lost. Jim is diagnosed with BPD.

Jim is an example of a BPD person in an identity crisis with unstable self-identity.

Identity defined:

Identity is similar to self-concept, self-esteem, self-awareness, self-confidence, self-satisfaction, and self-importance. One's self-identity is a combination of aspects depending on values such as:

--Artistic talent

--Knowledge

--Wealth

--Gender

--Hobbies

--Accomplishments

--Career

--Relationships

--Status and prestige

--Religion

--Values

--Priorities

--Physical appearance

--Health

--Place of residence

--Cultural affiliation

--Age

Identity development in early childhood:

During childhood one learns via genes and social experiences that others have different thoughts and ideas. And children acquire the ability to get what others are likely thinking and feeling.

Theory of mind:

Theory of mind is the theoretical mechanism that allows for self-reflection, identity development, and the ability to relate to others. Theory of mind is knowing that others think differently from you, and your understanding the psychological and emotional states of other people.

BPD people don't usually have a well developed theory of mind -- so they have trouble relating well to others.

In middle childhood from 6 to 12, children's identities develop along with their ability to regulate emotions. Along with identity development, children acquire skills in mastering school work, getting along well with others, and acquire basic mental and physical skills.

If they don't learn to regulate emotions along with the other skills, they can face adolescent turmoil, and impair their adult identity. BPD people may then have roller coaster emotions, volatile, and explosive anger if they can't regulate emotions.

Adolescent identity development:

Some psychologists refer to "possible selves" which refers to adolescents trying on different identities and discarding them. Adolescence can be stressful for most even if they don't have BPD. Pressures mount to establish a clear sense of identity in adolescence. So BPD people can find adolescence very difficult because they can't who they are in adulthood, let alone adolescence.

Fixing identity as an adult:

Normally people get through adolescence with a reasonably balanced sense of self. If one part of a healthy identity is threatened, a person can call on other parts to center himself.

For instance, a man is fired from a job. He can remind himself that he's a good parent to his kids, a good husband, and has many resources to bounce back and get a new job.

BPD & unstable, fragile identity:

People with BPD often overreact to minor threats to their shaky identities.

Shaky identities:

BPD people exhibit fluctuating attitudes, values, and feelings of identity.

Let's consider conflicting examples:

1) A normal man accepts a dinner invitation and dislikes the dinner. In order to not offend the host he says he enjoyed the dinner. He tells a little white lie. His reputation is honest and stable otherwise.

2) A woman with BPD goes to a dinner party, tells a white lie in saying she liked the food. However, the little lie she told results in her feeling a rush of self-loathing and disgust for her dishonest behavior. She is angry with her friend for inviting her to the dinner party. She can't hold onto her basic identity of being honest in the face of the minor lie.

3) A man with BPD views himself as righteous and devoted to his family, his wife, and kids. However, he frequently cheats on his wife, has affairs with other women, and loses his temper with his kids over the slightest, most minor issue. He rages and yells at his kids and wife, then feels guilty, and then snaps out of it. He's back to feeling righteous and devoted.

Many BPD people are chameleons, people pleasers, who change the facade of their identities to fit what they think others want. They try to personify their friends' or partners' dreams. But the instability of their identity makes keeping up the facade impossible.

Threats to identity:

When BPD people have their identities or self-worth threatened they may react in one of two ways:

1) They strike out in a rage to hold onto their fragile sense of self-worth.

2) Their identity and self-worth crumble and they fall into a cycle of despair and depression.

Examples:

A) A woman cheats on her husband. She may strike out at her husband and say, "It's your fault that I cheated. You never show me any affection." Or she may fall apart on the inside and tell herself, "I am a horrible person. I can't even be faithful to my husband."

B) If the identity concern is, "I am an inadequate parent." He may strike out in anger: "When you say that you wish the kids did better in school, you meant that I am a horrible parent. I could do a better job if you weren't so critical."

Alternatively, if he crumbles inside, he might say, "I'm so selfish. I should devote far more time to helping my kids with their schoolwork. What's wrong with me?"

C) The identity concern is: "I haven't ever accomplished what I should have." If he strikes out at his partner: "You don't make enough money! What's wrong with you? We'll always be broke!"

If he is shattered on the inside, he might say: "I'll never get anywhere. I don't have the discipline because of my mental illness. I'm hopeless."

Friends and partners of BPD people may be confused, angry, and mystified by the reaction because they don't understand the underlying identity problem that causes the reaction.

CHAPTER 22: INTERPERSONAL INSTABILITY & BPD

BPD people often have "rocky" relationships. Their intense emotions lead to relationships that are chaotic and out of control. Relationships can go great at one point or everything falls apart at another time.

The BPD person is in love, happy, and overjoyed one moment in a relationship. Then in the next moment he or she is angry, hateful, and hopeless about the relationship.

On the negative side relationships can escalate into serious conflicts, fights, and physical or emotional abuse. As with the emotional roller coaster, relationships can yo-yo up and down from great to awful.

--BPD, Perceptions & Boundaries:

If one is in a relationship with a BPD person, expect to get confusing, mixed-up communication and surprising emotional reactions.

BPD individuals have more broken relationships, more conflicts at work in getting along with others, and more arguments with friends and relatives than others. They have a lack of skills to get perspective on situations from others' viewpoint.

The skill to stand back requires these abilities they lack:

1) Lack skills to get needs, feelings, beliefs of others

2) Lack skills to see how others perceive them

3) Lack skills to see how their own behavior impacts others

Not getting other people's needs, feelings, and perspectives causes BPD people to cross others' boundaries. The usual BPD problem is that they put excessive demands on people and have a sense of entitlement. So they demand special treatment and get angry if they don't get all they want.

--Taking Others' Viewpoint:

When one can take a panoramic view and have insights into others' views, feelings, and needs, it helps with relationships, success at work and school. Of course, comprehension of others' perspectives varies with the time and life stressors involved.

For example, driver A waits for a parking spot. Driver B hits driver A's car from behind because he wanted the parking space. It is likely that driver A will be short of empathy for driver B.

How do BPD people do taking the bird's-eye view regarding others?

--Insights into Others:

Sometimes BPD people pick up on others feelings. But they don't get the why behind their feelings or what their feelings mean.

Here's an example of Joe who has BPD vs. Jillian his girlfriend:

Joe comes home from work at dinnertime and finds Jillian, his girlfriend, stretched out on the couch watching a football game on TV. He asks her what's for dinner. She's absorbed in the football game and ignores him.

"Earth to Jillian," Joe says, raising his voice. "You're tuning me out."

"What, honey?" Jillian answers.

"I asked what's for dinner!" Joe snaps.

"Just fix yourself a sandwich," Jillian replies.

"Don't you care enough about me to fix a dinner? Like steak, mashed potatoes, veggies and dessert?" Joe asks in an agitated voice.

"Joe, I'm in the middle of a real exciting football game!"

"So some ball game is more important than me and dinner?" Joe yells.

"Come on, give me a break, sweetie," Jillian calls out. "What's the emergency?"

"I getcha," Joe growls. "Some crap on TV beats the hell out of addressing my needs."

"Your needs?"

"The hell with you," Joe barks. "Watch your TV. I'll starve to death!"

Jillian knows it is pointless to argue in circles with Joe. Joe storms off into the bathroom and slams the door.

Joe correctly realized Jillian was distracted by TV. But he misinterprets her focus on football on TV as a personal insult to him. And he exaggerates that she is aiming to let him starve to death.

He only sees part of her perspective in noticing she is preoccupied by TV. Joe makes intimacy with Jillian impossible by being blind to most of her viewpoint.

--You via Others' Viewpoint:

People with BPD can show problematic behavior, emotional outbursts, and view themselves as quite reasonable and logical. Yet others see their behavior as outrageous and controlling such as:

1) Jealousy & BPD:

Fear of abandonment drives some BPD people into such intense jealousy that they call their partners excessively, constantly seeking reassurance, and checking up on their partners' every move.

For example, in *Fatal Attraction*, Alex Forrest (Glenn Close) is a BPD type who stalks Dan Gallagher (Michael Douglas) after they have a one-weekend stand, a brief affair while Dan's wife is away. He shrugs off the affair as a mistake and considers it over.

But Alex won't be ignored. Not now, not tomorrow, not ever... even if it means destroying Dan's family to keep him. Alex doesn't understand that behaviors like hers scare people and drive them away.

2) Seductiveness & BPD:

Without being aware of the impact on others, many BPD people engage in sexualized, seductive gestures, facial expressions, touches, and use a sexy voice.

Then they act shocked, offended, or even outraged when others respond with sexual advances. And they may be involved in cheating affairs while they are jealous of their partners.

As an illustration consider comments Marilyn Monroe made:

"Sometimes I've got such lousy taste in men... There were times when I'd... run into one of these Hollywood heels at a party and they'd paw me cheaply in front of everybody as if they were saying, 'Oh, we had her.' I guess it's the classic situation of an ex-whore, though I was never a whore in that sense. I was never kept. I always kept myself."

Marilyn seems to have zero insight into her seductive behavior -- she wore tight-fitting, sexy clothes, spoke in a seductive tone of voice, and went to great efforts to move seductively. She'd transform herself into this sexy creature in a kind of hysteric trance and then she was shocked when some guy came on to her.

Marilyn continues complaining on how men hit on her:

"But there was a period when I responded too much to flattery and slept around too much, thinking it would help my career, though I always liked the guy at the time. They were always so full of self-confidence and I had none at all and they made me feel better."

3) Anger & BPD:

Because of the typical angry outbursts from a lot of BPD people, others tend to avoid them or approach them with trepidation which the BPD type can't understand.

For example:

Harry rented a guest cottage from an estate owner. The landlord's wife was a classic BPD person without any sense of boundaries or tenants' rights. She'd show up at all hours with no notice and peep into Harry's windows, demand to be let in the cottage, and lecture Harry on how to clean the cottage.

One week she left 16 pages of notes on how to clean the cottage. She'd demand that Harry give her rides in his car into town so she could run errands, go shopping or whatever. When Harry tried to set boundaries, refused to give her free rides to town, and objected to her constant visits, she'd throw temper tantrums, scream, and throw things.

Then the landlord would warn Harry to be nice to his wife as if this was all Harry's fault. The next day after her outbursts she'd show up as if nothing had happened and give Harry more unsolicited advice, control-freak notes on cleaning, and tell him how to live his life. She didn't get why everybody ran when she approached them.

4) Hysteria & BPD:

People with BPD tend to wildly overreact with intense emotion to minor everyday stressors. As in the last example, the rich man's BPD wife verbally abused Harry, the tenant, because he would not give her a ride to town.

She exploded with anger and threw a horrendous temper tantrum like a two-year-old demanding candy. Logically, she could call a taxi or have her husband drive her since she didn't like to drive. But to her, her sense of entitlement was violated and so she became hysterical.

Here are examples of the BPD person's usual hysteria type reactions:

A) Irritation turns to rage

B) Sadness turns into major depression or profound dysphoria -- a generalized feeling of distress

C) Simple pleasure morphs into ecstasy and incredible joy

D) Worry transforms into terror

5) Impulsivity & BPD:

BPD people can get into impulsivity that's self-destructive such as self-mutilation, suicide attempts, threats, out-of-control spending, substance abuse, etc. They can't put brakes on their behavior.

--Unintended Pain:

Because BPD people are so focused on their own emotional distress and turmoil, they fail to see the painful impact they have on others. The ability to get others' viewpoint is key to getting along in relationships.

Insight into how others feel and think will enable a person to relate to friends, colleagues, and lovers. Usually BPD people are not intentionally trying to hurt themselves or others, they just don't have the perspective on others thoughts and feelings.

Consider the case of Helen and Tom who were married for 20 years. For years Helen complained about her BPD husband, Tom, who was abusive and hurting her emotionally. Her therapist asked her why she didn't leave Tom and divorce him.

"Because of the children," she replied.

One day her teenage daughter asked her, "Mom, why do you stay with Dad when he's so mean to you?"

"I do it for you," Helen said.

It finally sunk into Helen's thick skull that she wasn't doing her children a favor by taking abuse from Tom and volunteering to be a victim, allowing Tom to hurt her. Helen had become more and more withdrawn, afraid, hurt, and angry at Tom.

After 20 years of hurt and abuse she finally divorced him. Tom's mind was so totally immersed in his own misery that he could not see the hurt he was causing his wife, Helen.

--Crashing Boundaries:

Like fences around properties, people have personal boundaries setting rules, limits, expectations, and even personal space that people are comfortable with. People with BPD don't understand or respect other people's boundaries. The BPD type might make a social call in the middle of the night to disturb a new friend. Or call a new love interest too often.

For example, in *The King of Comedy* film, Rupert Pupkin (De Niro), an aspiring stand-up comic, stalks and crosses the boundaries of Jerry Langford (Jerry Lewis), a talk show host on TV. Pupkin, uninvited, jumps into Langford's limo outside his TV studio. He insists on pitching Langford on his stand-up comedy act -- he asks to go on Langford's TV talk show. Langford humors Pupkin and brushes him off.

Pupkin busts through more of Langford's boundaries by crashing his way into Langford's TV show offices with his audition tape. Next he takes a date and talks his way into Jerry Langford's home in the suburbs outside New York City. When Jerry arrives home he throws Rupert out and refuses to listen to his comedy tape.

Next Rupert and his wacky sidekick (Sandra Bernard) kidnap Jerry and hold him hostage. Rupert forces his way onto Jerry's TV show and gets his shot on Jerry's show. Rupert then is arrested by the FBI and spends a couple years in prison. Rupert is so obsessed by the idea of a TV shot to kick off his stand-up comic career, he crosses Jerry's boundaries, kidnaps him at gunpoint, and ends up in prison.

--Partners & Lovers Boundaries:

The paradox that the BPD person puts in motion is that the more he/she disrespects the boundaries of a partner or lover the more likely they will be abandoned. By demanding to know where the partner or lover is at all times and subjecting them to cross-examinations or inquisitions, they drive them away which is what they were trying to prevent.

Laurel Canyon, a movie starring Christian Bale as a nutty, BPD type psychiatrist, presents the Bale character as over-controlling his bride-to-be played by Kate Beckinsale. The irony is while the Bale character cheats on his lover (Beckinsale), he warns her to stay away from his mother's free-spirited musician clients.

This disrespecting his lover's boundaries results in her playing around with a rock band member and a dramatic confrontation when he catches her in a seductive compromise with another man.

--Friends & Co-workers vs. BPD People:

While living in the eye of a hurricane, the BPD person may push friends into intervene on their behalf. They may set up conflicts between friends and acquaintances.

The BPD type may put special demands on their employer by:

A) Asking for special treatment

B) Requesting hour changes

C) Asking for additional time off

D) Asking for private meetings

E) Demand special considerations by claiming some esoteric illness they don't really have

F) Spread rumors about co-workers and spoil the atmosphere at work

--Doctors & Therapists vs. BPD Types:

What About Bob? Is a movie comedy with Bill Murray playing Bob, a BPD type character, who strains relations with his psychiatrist played by Richard Dreyfuss.

Bob is a mental patient who is very afraid of abandonment. So when his doctor takes a vacation with his family, Bob stalks him. Bob manages to charm the doctor's wife and kids while driving his doctor crazy with special demands combined with crashing boundaries.

BPD clients may frequently make special demands and cross professional boundaries. When professional clinicians have many BPD clients they can easily feel overwhelmed by a range of demands their clients make.

BPD types may do the following:

1) Asking for special appointment times

2) Cancel at the last minute

3) Seem overly friendly and personal

4) Behave seductively

5) Call after hours

6) Make ending a session hard

7) Expect discounts or special financial deals

8) Expect special help from providers

9) Ask inappropriate personal questions

10) Demand special medications they think they need

--Kids' Boundaries & BPD Parents:

Parents with BPD may cross boundaries in various ways with their children. They may fear losing the love of their kids and try to be the best friends of their kids -- instead of being the guides or leaders that kids need. By becoming overly involved with their kids they frustrate their kids' development.

Examples include the following:

1) Complete or do their kids' homework

2) Blaming authority figures when their kids are in trouble

3) Starting arguments with their kids' friends and/or parents

4) Overly intrusive -- asking their kids to reveal almost every detail of their lives

Such over-involvement is sometimes termed *enmeshment* -- referring to the difficulty the BPD parent has in respecting others' lives vs. their own.

The unintended consequence of enmeshed parents is that children have trouble with:

1) Accomplishing the basic tasks of childhood and adolescence

2) Can't easily form a clear, individual identity

3) Have problems acquiring the ability to function autonomously

On the opposite side, some BPD parents fail to set boundaries with their kids by withdrawing, isolating, retreating, and becoming underinvolved. These parents may fail to set rules and neglect to provide love, attention, and support to their children.

When parents don't set appropriate structures, the children don't learn critical societal rules, and end up vulnerable to emotional problems later in life.

After their children become adults, BPD parents may continue to disrespect their kids boundaries. For instance, the parents may constantly give unsolicited advice regarding their kids relationships, lives, and finances.

Or they may ask their adult kids for advice on their relationships, go to their kids for financial or emotional support.

Many TV sitcoms frequently use parent characters who are BPD types for a laugh. In the *Seinfeld* episode *The Stake Out*, Jerry enters his apartment to find his parents under the covers on Jerry's folded-out sofa bed. Jerry starts asking his parents dumb questions to setup the boundary crossing.

His parents then give him unsolicited advice about his romantic life:

Jerry: How many people work at these big law offices?

Father: Depends on the firm.

Jerry: Yeah, but if you called up and described someone, do you think they would know who it was?

Father: What's the matter? You need a lawyer?

Jerry: No. I met someone at this party and I know where she works but I don't know her name.

Mother: So, why don't you ask someone who was at the party?

Jerry: No, the only one I could ask is Elaine and I can't ask her.

Father: Why not?

Jerry: Because it's complicated. There's some tension there.

Mother: He used to go with her.

Father: Which one is she?

Mother: From Maryland. The one that brought the chocolate covered cherries you didn't like.

Father: Oh, yeah, very alert... warm person.

Jerry: Oh, yeah, she's great.

Mother: So how come nothing materialized there?

Jerry: Well, it's a tough thing to talk about, uh, I don't know.

Mother: I know what it was.

Jerry: You don't know what it was.

Mother: So, what was it?

Jerry: Well, we would fight a lot, for some reason.

Mother: Oh... well.

Father: Oh... well.

Jerry: And, there was a little problem with the physical chemistry.

A *stunned silence -- everyone is uncomfortable.*

Mother: Well, I think she's a very attractive girl.

Jerry: Oh, she is... she absolutely is.

Mother: I can see if there was a weight problem.

Jerry: No, it's not that. It wasn't all one-sided.

Mother: You know, you can't be so particular. Nobody's perfect.

Jerry: I know. I know.

Father: (Going for the joke) You know, Jerry, it's a good thing I wasn't so particular.

Mother: Idiot. (To Jerry) So, who are you looking for, Sophia Loren?

Jerry: That's got nothing to do with it.

Father: How about Loni Anderson?

Mother: Where do you get Loni Anderson?

Father: Why, what's wrong with Loni Anderson?

Mother: I like Elaine more than Loni Anderson.

Jerry: What are you two talking about? Look, Elaine just wasn't the one.

Mother: And this other one's the one?

Jerry: I don't know, maybe.

Father: So ask Elaine there for the number.

Jerry: I can't. She'll get upset. I never talk about other women with her, especially this one tonight.

Mother: How could you still see her if you're not interested?

Jerry: We're friends.

Father: Doesn't sound like you're friends to me. If you were friends, you'd... you'd ask her for the number. Do you know where this other one works?

Jerry: Oh yeah.

Father: So go up to the office.

Mother: Up to her office?

Father: Go to the building. She goes out to lunch, doesn't she?

Jerry: I guess.

Father: So you stand in the lobby by the elevator and wait for her to come down for lunch.

Jerry: You mean stake out the lobby?

Mother: Oh, Morty, that's ridiculous. Just ask Elaine for the number.

Father: He doesn't want to ask Elaine for the number.

Mother: So, you've got him standing by the elevator like a dope. What happens when he sees her?

Father: He pretends he bumped into her.

Jerry: You know what? That is not that bad an idea.

Fade out.

Jerry's parents act like BPD parents who don't understand why their son sets boundaries. Because they can't take Jerry's perspective they don't respect his boundaries. Of course, depending on your sense of humor, this is suppose to be funny.

CHAPTER 23: EXTREME THINKING & BPD

BPD people tend toward extreme thinking and some theorists refer to "schemas" or powerful beliefs BPD people have as part of the cause for their turbulent lives. Schemas can be divided into healthy, middle ground schemas and disruptive, extreme schemas.

How you see the world:

Schemas are like glasses that:

1) Help you see the world more clearly or...

2) Schemas can show you a blurred, cracked, grotesquely distorted vision of the world

Development of schemas:

Schemas start forming in childhood. They're influenced by parents, caregivers, peers, teachers, and relatives. Other influences on schema development include life events, illnesses, tragic accidents, and genetic predispositions.

Incompetent schema:

As an example of developing an incompetent schema, Billy grew up helping his father at various tasks. His father always abused him verbally, yelling, "Billy, you're stupid and clumsy." So Billy grew up feeling incompetent. He didn't bother to try to do his school work because his father convinced him he was stupid and incompetent.

Competent schema:

Mary, however, was raised by loving parents who encouraged her. She was praised for good work and gently corrected when needed. When she got a B instead of an A on a school test, her parents told her that was okay.

It was a good learning experience. Through trial and error she could learn something. Her schema of competence grows as she meets challenges in school work, for instance, because of her parents' constructive approach to her development.

Some types of schemas:

1) Self-concept schemas: Who am I? Am I capable? What am I worth?

2) Relationship schemas: Can I trust others or should I avoid them? How do I deserve to be treated, and how should I treat others?

3) World schemas: Is the world safe or dangerous? Predictable or unpredictable?

Opposites and middle-ground schemas:

Schemas develop like other concepts from getting opposites such as beautiful vs. ugly, hot vs. cold, sad vs. happy. The middle-ground schema between hot and cold is lukewarm. In schemas the middle-ground position is one of competence.

Take the example of Tom, Dick, and Harry:

A) Tom holds a belief, attitude or schema in his mind of incompetence. When faced with a difficulty he feels inadequate, overwhelmed, and incapable of solving the problem.

B) Dick has an opposite schema of omnipotence -- he can do anything. He'll take on any problem by himself even if he needs help.

C) Harry has a schema in the middle of competence. With a competence schema, Harry carefully considers a problem, gets help when needed.

Four reasons why schemas are hard to change:

1) Schemas act like filters:

If a person has a schema of inferiority, the schema tends to filter out contrary information. For example, if Tony has a schema of inferiority he tends to ignore or discount evidence that shows he has more potential or competence.

If he gets a raise at work or a great grade at school on a project, he will ignore it or discount it assuming he is incompetent or inferior compared with to others around him. If Tony has a schema that the world is a very dangerous place, the presence of a security guard or a cop in a dark parking lot will not reassure him or be enough.

2) Schemas encourage misinterpretation:

George, for instance, has an "anxious attachment" schema (an intense fear that people will leave him or abandon him). So when George goes to a party with his girlfriend, he gets very anxious when his girlfriend circulates without him. He interprets her actions as evidence that she is looking for another guy to replace George. So he makes an effort to stay close to her and watch her.

3) Schemas lead to fear:

Betty has an inferiority schema and so she's afraid to challenge her schema because of the consequences of failure. So she avoids trying to perform at anything.

Betty also has a schema of idealizing. She idealizes her husband. He's perfect. So when he is out at suspicious times and is cheating on her, she does not want to ask questions and find out things she doesn't want to know.

4) Schemas are invisible:

Schemas are invisible and people are not aware that they have schemas dictating how they see reality. Thus, you can't change something you don't know exists.

Therapy & new experiences:

While schemas don't easily change, over a period of years with new experiences and/or therapy one can change schemas for the better.

Extreme thinking in BPD people:

BPD people usually think in extremes such as all black or all white -- no grays. This is called "splitting" by some theorists -- the difficulty of finding a middle "gray" ground.

Pete, for example, has extreme schemas of "undeserving" or "entitled" -- no middle ground of a "deserved" schema. So Pete feels undeserving when something good happens. Yet when his wife fails to pick up groceries he asked for, he flips-out into a rage feeling entitled to the food items he demanded. He accuses her of not caring about him. The wife said she got caught in traffic and had to pick up the kids from school.

Another man, without BPD, confronted by the same situation would be sympathetic with his wife's situation. He has a schema of "deserving" and views the inconvenience differently.

Some of the common schemas include self-concept schemas, relationship schemas, and world schemas. Each has maladaptive positions at the extremes and adaptive points at the middle-ground position.

Self-Concept Schemas:

Personal schemas are called "self-concept schemas" by schema theorists. They influence what you do, feel, and expect in life. You develop schemas through experience and early interactions with caregivers in childhood.

BPD people have two dimensions of self-concept schemas including the extremes of entitled self-concept schema vs. undeserving self-concept schema.

1) Entitled vs. undeserving:

The BPD person with an entitled schema type demands what he wants when he wants it. This entitled type attitude leads to demands at the drop of a hat, instantly, and feeling rage if he doesn't get his way. The entitled BPD person does not care about the needs of others.

At the opposite dimension, the undeserved schema BPD holder expects to not get his needs met. He does not deserve it. So he doesn't expect attention or consideration from others. They don't ask for what they want and so their needs go unmet.

BPD people often flip from the extremes of entitled to undeserving. As an illustration, Jane goes to a restaurant and gets enraged by slow service from her waiter. Jane throws a temper tantrum and makes a scene at the restaurant.

The waiter apologizes and says he's new on the job and they are short of wait staff because two waiters are out sick. Jane then is overwhelmed with shame for her outburst of anger and suddenly she feels undeserving of any kindness.

"Balanced self-worth" is the middle-ground schema. A person with a "balanced self-worth" expects to have his needs met but not at the cost of others feelings or all the time. They balance their needs vs. those of others.

How do extreme schemas develop? Unbalanced, maladaptive parenting can cause the development of extreme schemas in BPD people. For instance, if parents spoil their kids the children may grow up with a sense of entitlement. If parents neglect and abuse a child, he may grow up with a problematic, undeserving or inferiority schema.

2) Inferiority vs. superiority:

With "inferiority schemas", the BPD person feels inadequate compared to others, has no confidence in his abilities and talents, gives up easily, and thus has a self-fulfilling prophecy leading to more feeling of incompetence.

The reverse is the BPD individual with a "superiority schema" who believe they're brighter and better than others. People like this are "narcissistic" or extremely self-centered. They may pursue goals at any cost at the expense of others who don't show up on their radar.

The BPD person may flip from superiority schema to inferiority schema. Sam, BPD person, had risen to head a hedge fund on Wall Street in New York City. He got used to big multi-million dollar bonuses each year.

After ten years he had a bad year, lost many millions of the firm's money, and was fired. He couldn't get another similar financial job. Sam then flips over to an inferiority schema because he can't pay his bills or support his family.

"Self-acceptance" is a middle-ground schema which includes accurate beliefs about oneself. The middle-ground person realizes that he's not superior or inferior and than people have different sets of skills and talents.

Development of the maladaptive extreme schemas comes likely from parenting mistakes. If the parent harshly criticizes a child for failures, he can develop an inferiority schema. If parents over-praise or pile on unearned rewards for a child then he can develop a superiority schema which causes problems as the child grows up.

3) Self-concept schemas in action:

Marty developed a superiority schema in childhood because his father, Bill, spoiled him with material things, sporting items, etc. Marty felt a sense of entitlement from his father's financial gifts. Then Bill got caught dealing drugs and went to prison. Marty's mother was only able to afford a bare essentials lifestyle suddenly.

Marty felt ashamed, switched over to feeling inferior and avoided his old friends and never talked about his family. As Marty grew into adulthood, he found he could not keep a minimum-wage job for more than two months.

Because early in childhood Marty developed superiority and entitlement schemas, he set himself up for a fall when he ran into failure. He moved to the opposite extreme of undeserving and inferior. Inflated schemas are punctured by negative events.

Relationship Schemas:

Good or bad relationships or friendships are set up by the development of various relationship schemas. Two extreme types apply to BPD people: anxious attachment vs. avoidant attachment and idealizing vs. demonizing.

1) Anxious attachment vs. avoidant attachment:

BPD people with an "anxious attachment schema" have a great fear of being abandoned or rejected. So they tend to be clingy, jealous, and sensitive to possible rejection signs. Their overly sensitive, jealousy-driven behaviors, and assuming the worst about a partner or lover can lead to the abandonment they fear.

The other extreme, BPD people with an "avoidant-attachment schema" isolate and stay away from others. They don't want people in their lives who may hurt them. They end up seeming aloof and uninterested in others.

For example, Carrie's mother, Susan, operates from an anxious attachment schema viewpoint. Carrie is an adult. Susan calls Carrie several times a day and stops by to visit her uninvited. Susan over-shares details of her life. The mother is doing this because of her anxious attachment which reassures her that her daughter loves her.

Finally, Carrie is fed up and sets boundaries -- she tells her mother she may call her once a week and not visit unless invited. Her mother throws a fit, rages at her daughter for being ungrateful, and flips into an avoidant attachment schema. Susan does not call or visit Carrie for six months.

"Secure-attachment schema" is the middle-ground schema. Friendships are formed on the basis of mutual caring and respect. People with "secure-attachment schemas" as a guide tend to evaluate new people and relationships without being overly distrusting or naive. They don't sabotage the relationship with jealous or clingy behaviors.

Development of problematic schemas -- such as anxious-attachment schemas or avoidant-attachment schemas -- can result from weak parenting practices. Parents who abuse or neglect their children may set them up for extreme attachment problems. And control-freak parents who enmesh themselves in their kids' lives, who try to control and dictate every move, can also cause troublesome schemas in their kids as they grow up.

2) Idealizing vs. demonization:

Many BPD people tend toward using an "idealized schema" and project that their partners, lovers, or friends are all good with no faults. So holding people to such high standards means that they'll disappoint them.

"Demonizing schema" is using an extremely negative view of others. Everybody is malicious and out to get them. They don't trust anybody because everybody is hostile and evil.

There are scenes in the movie *Manhattan* which illustrate the demonizing schema. Ike (Woody Allen), who is about 40, is on a date with Tracy (Mariel Hemingway), his 17-year-old girlfriend, when he runs into his buddy, Yale (Michael Murphy), 40s, who is cheating on his wife with his date, Mary (Diane Keaton), about 30. Ike, who is somewhat of a BPD type, starts demonizing Mary in his mind as she expresses her opinions:

Yale: Mary and I have invented the, uh, Academy of the Overrated--

Mary: That's right. (*She laughs*)

Yale: --for, uh, such notables as...

Mary: Such people as, uh...

Yale: (*Laughing*) Gustav Mahler.

Mary: And Isak Denisen and Carl Jung...

Yale: Scott Fitzgerald and... (*Chuckling*) uh--

Mary: Lenny Bruce. We can't forget Lenny Bruce-- now, can we?

Yale: (*Laughing*) *Lenny Bruce.*

Mary: And how about Norman Mailer and Walt Whitman and--

Ike: I think those people are all terrific, everyone that you mentioned.

Mary: What? What?

Yale: (*To Mary*) Who's that guy you had? You had a great one last week.

Mary: No, no, I didn't have it. It was yours. It was Heinrich Boll, wasn't it?

Yale: (*Laughing*) Oh, God.

Ike: (*Looking incredulous*) Overrated?

Yale: Anyway, we don't wanna leave out ol' Heinrich.

Ike: Hey, what about Mozart? You guys don't wanna leave out Mozart -- I mean, while you're trashing people.

Mary: (*Chuckling*) Oh, well, how about Vincent Van Gogh (*Pronouncing it "Goch"*) ...or Ingmar Bergman?

Ike: Van Goch? (Aside to Tracy) Did she say "Van Goch"?

Mary: How about Ingmar Bergman?

Ike: (*Shaking his head*) Van Goch?

Yale: (*To Mary*) Oh, you -- you'll get in trouble with Bergman. (*He sighs*)

Mary: What do you mean?

Ike: Bergman? Bergman's the only genius in cinema today, I think. I just mean--

Yale: He's a big Bergman fan, you know.

Mary: (*Looking at Ike, gesturing*) Oh, please, you know. God, you're so the opposite! I mean, you write that absolutely fabulous television show. It's brilliantly funny and his view is so Scandinavian. It's bleak, my God. I mean, all that Kierkegaard, right? Real adolescent, you know, fashionable pessimism. I mean, the silence. God's silence. Okay, okay, okay, I mean, I loved it when I was at Radcliffe, but, I mean, all right, you outgrow it. You absolutely outgrow it.

Yale: Ah, I think I've got to go with him and Ingmar. (*He laughs hesitantly*)

Ike: (*Aside to Tracy*) Get her away from me. I don't think I can take too much more of her. She's really a cr-creep.

Mary: Oh, no, no, no, no, don't you see -- don't you guys see that it is the dignifying of one's own psychological and sexual hangups by attaching them to these grandiose philosophical issues? That's what it is.

Ike clears his throat. The group stops walking.

Yale: (*Pointing to a nearby apartment building*) Here we are.

Ike: (*Fumbling*) Uh, listen, I...

Mary: Oh.

Ike: (*To Mary*) It was very nice meeting you.

Mary: Well.

Ike: (*Shaking Mary's hand*) It was -- it was a pleasure and a--

Yale: Oh.

Ike: --sincere sensation, but we have to go--

Mary: Yeah, well.

Ike: --because we gotta get some -- we gotta do some shopping. I forgot about it.

Mary: (*Laughing nervously*) Hey, listen. Hey, listen, I don't even wanna have this conversation. I mean -- really, I mean, I'm just from Philadelphia. You know, I mean, we believe in God, so -- uh, uh, okay?

Ike: (*Gesturing*) What the hell does that mean?

Mary: (*Frowning, confused*) Is it?

Ike: (*Gesturing*) What is it -- what -- what'd you -- what'd you -- what'd she mean -- what do you mean by that there?

Mary: Well, what--

Ike: "I'm from Philadelphia... I believe in God." What -- what does... (*Mary laughs nervously*) Does -- does this make any sense to you at all? I...

Interior. Deli.

Tracy and Ike are picking up some groceries. While Tracy calmly looks at the foodstuff, a wire basket in her hand, Ike talks and gestures rapidly.

Ike: (*Sighing*) What a creep! Could you believe her? I mean, she was really--

Tracy: Oh, she seemed real nervous.

Ike: Nervous? She was overbearing. She was, mm, you know, mm, terrible. She was all cerebral (*Sighing and pointing to his head*) you know. Wh-was -- where the hell does that little Radcliffe tootsie come off rating, mm, Scott Fitzgerald and Gustav Mahler and then Heinrich Boll?

Tracy: (*Putting a can in her basket*) I don't understand why you're getting so mad.

Ike: I'm mad because I don't like that pseudointellectual garbage. And she was pedantic. Van Gogh. (*Pronouncing it "Goch"*) Did you hear that? She said "Van Goch." I couldn't-- Like an Arab she spoke. I couldn't... and if she had made one more remark about Bergman, I would've knocked her other contact lens out.

He makes a fist in the air.

Tracy: Oh, is she Yale's mistress?

Ike: (*Shaking his head*) That will never cease to mystify me. I mean, he's got a wonderful wife and he prefers to -- to, mm, diddle this little yo-yo that -- that... you know. Uh, but -- he was always a sucker for, uh, th-th-those kind of women, you know, the kind, uh, who'd involve him in discussions of existential reality, you know. They probably sit around the floor with wine and cheese and mispronounce "allegorical" and "didacticism."

He sighs.

Ike, as if he had a BPD demonization schema, demonizes the Mary character. In a contrary action later, he jumps at the chance to start dating Mary himself when Yale drops her. Then Ike acts like he's idealizing her. He rejects Tracy and jumps into a relationship with Mary.

Showing that Ike has had dysfunctional, unstable relationships, he goes to pick up his son from his second ex-wife who left him for a woman. It is revealed that he was stalking and peeping through cabin windows at Jill (Meryl Streep), his ex-wife, and her lesbian lover, Connie. Ike tried to kill Connie by running her over with a car.

Later, Yale dumps his wife and goes off with Mary who rejects Ike. Ike tries to get Tracy back but she's flying off to London. Ike flips back to demonizing both Mary and Yale. He confronts both of them for betraying him. Of course, Manhattan is a sort of a dark comedy. But Ike's BPD comes across.

As if Ike's unstable relationship issue isn't enough, he angrily fights with his co-workers on a TV show and quits:

Ike: Why do you think it's funny?

Paul: (*Gesturing*) Look at the audience.

Ike: That's not a--

Dick: (*Pointing to the audience below the control booth*) Look at -- look at the audience there.

Ike: (*Listening to the audience laughter coming from the monitor*) You're going by the -- you're going by audience reaction to this? I mean, this is an audience that's raised on television. Their -- their standards have been systematically lowered over the years. You know, these guys sit in front of their sets and the -- the gamma rays eat the white cells of their brains out. Uh, you know, um, ya, I'm-- I quit.

He stands up and leans over the console, picking up his jacket from a chair.

Dick: All right. Just relax. Take a lude. Take a lude.

Ike: No, no, no, no, no, I quit. I can't write this anymore. I can't... I don't want a lude.

The men in the control booth are quiet for a brief moment; the audience laughter and the interview dialogue continues over the monitor in the silence.

Ike: (*Putting on his jacket and breaking the pause*) All you guys do is -- is, uh, drop ludes and then -- then take Percodans and angel dust. Naturally, it seems funny.

Dick: You know, just relax, relax.

Ike: (*Gesturing*) Anything would if you're -- if you're... You know, we, y-y-you should abandon the show and open up a pharmaceutical house.

He storms off quitting his job and putting himself in a financial bind. Ike has demonized his co-workers, the audience, and his writing job.

BPD people often flip their attitude toward others from one extreme to the other. For instance, they see a friend or partner as perfect. Soon the idealized other lets them down in some way. Then they demonize that person. When at the demon status level, any flaw then reinforces the demonization.

"Realistic-view schema" is the middle-ground. A person sees another as neither all good or all bad. He expects others to have positive traits and some weaknesses as we all do. So as one experiences ups and downs with friends, the relationship can endure through better or worse.

Development of extreme schemas of "idealizing" vs. "demonizing" is promoted by parental errors. If the parent tells the child the world is out to hurt them then a demonizing schema develops. If parents present a naive, Pollyanna-style view of others, then an idealizing schema develops. BPD people see others in extremes then of demons or angels.

3) Relationship schemas in action:

Walt, 25, has an unstable, rocky relationship with his girlfriend, Sally. He flips from an anxious attachment schema to an avoidant attachment schema. On top of that he jumps from demonizing and idealizing schemas which further complicates his relationship with his girlfriend.

Walt, a BPD type, has a session with his therapist:

Walt: My girlfriend, Sally, is driving me crazy. She's insulting me and getting ready to dump me.

Doctor: Why do you say that?

Walt: She basically called me a pimp or a male whore.

Doctor: What did she say? What happened?

Walt: I fixed my brother up with a date. We were on a double date with my brother, Jim, who is 21 -- same age as Sally. She said Jim should find his own dates. And she keeps talking about Jim because she says he had a steady job. I can't help being unemployed. There's high unemployment in my industry -- sales jobs are hard to get.

Doctor: So how do you get to "pimp" and "male whore"?

Walt: Sally was critical of me for having a string of girlfriends and jobs -- nothing sticks for more than a few months. Sally's sounding like my last girlfriend who dumped me for a richer guy.

Doctor: But you're still together, right?

Walt: I get the feeling she's gonna shitcan me -- reject me soon. I'm going to beat her to the punch and dump her first. Then I'm gonna stop dating women for a long time. Sally's turned into a bitch flirting with my brother. My goddamn brother's a bird-dog. He'll be sleeping with Sally behind my back soon.

Doctor: Where is the evidence for this scenario?

Walt: I'm picking up on the cues from Sally. She was too friendly to my brother on the double date.

Doctor: What's too friendly mean?

Walt: Laughing like a hyena at Jim's jokes, giving him seductive looks. I was so pissed at her I passed up going to bed with her last night. I'm not gonna see her again.

Walt has gone from an anxious-attachment schema, being suspicious of Sally and fearing she'll abandon him, to an avoidant-attachment solution. He then demonizes Sally and his brother to justify jumping to conclusions. Walt feels jealous of any attention Sally gave his brother Jim. And without justification goes from one extreme to the other.

World Schemas:

BPD people often experience two schema dimensions -- dangerous vs. totally safe, and unpredictable vs. totally predictable.

1) Dangerous vs. totally safe:

People who see the world through a dangerous schema tend to be hypervigilant, take precautions, and see the world as a jungle.

Alternatively, those who see the world through a totally-safe schema take unnecessary risks and show clueless naivete.

"Reasonably safe" is the middle ground schema -- people viewing the world through the reasonably-safe schema avoid the paranoid approach. But they take appropriate precautions.

Development may result from abusive parents who raise their kids to feel continual fear -- the dangerous schema develops. While children who are overprotected by their parents view the world through a totally-safe schema and have no fears.

2) Unpredictable vs. totally predictable:

BPD people with an unpredictable schema see the world as chaotic, don't develop a life plan because they don't think plans ever work out. They are pessimistic, see themselves as victims, feel overwhelmed and helpless.

If one sees the world from the opposite dimension -- totally predictable -- then they may feel they're masters of their fate, the world will bend to their will, and that they don't need a Plan B. One plan will take care of their careers, investments, and relationships. However, when things don't go their way they tend to fall apart.

"Predictable schema" represents the middle-ground, the sensible approach that outcomes have some predictability. But they realize that nobody controls all the variables. They are ready for life's curve balls, frustrations, and have not only a Plan A, but a Plan B, and Plan C.

The development of kids that leads to the unpredictable schema is a result of families ruled by chaos. Some childhoods have more than their share of unpredictable, uncontrollable events, such as deaths, divorces, job losses, abuse, and neglect.

At the other end of the spectrum there are some parents who plan every detail of their kids' lives -- what they'll do and with whom they'll do it. These kids who never face an unplanned situation typically end up with totally-predictable schemas.

3) World schemas in action:

People with BPD tend to have extreme schemas and react with intense emotions and freak out over bumps in the road of life. Let's consider two people -- Vince who has BPD and Meg who doesn't.

Vince and Meg are teachers working in a school. Meg has reasonably safe and predictable schemas. Vince views the world through dangerous and unpredictable schemas.

A fire alarm goes off. Vince yells, "The school's on fire. Everybody run!" Vince's class starts running into the hall.

Meg calls the office and finds out it was a false alarm. She tells her class to stay in their seats and that it is a false alarm. Meg goes into the hall and yells at Vince that it is a false alarm. Vince rounds up his class and takes them back into his classroom.

Vince hit the panic button and did not wait for a confirmation. Meg checked and found it was a false alarm. Meg helped save Vince and his class from wasting school time running around the building.

CHAPTER 24:   DISSOCIATION, PARANOIA & BPD

When people with BPD get stressed-out, they can experience negative thinking, paranoid thoughts, and disconnection from self or reality -- this is called "cognitive dysregulation".

Paranoid or suspicious thoughts includes the idea that one is being followed, plotted against, talked about, persecuted, etc. Dissociation is an abnormal psychological state in which one's perception of oneself and/or one's environment is altered significantly.

Because somebody is suspicious, has negative, or "paranoid" thinking about others' motives, it doesn't mean they are delusional, schizophrenic, or psychotic. It means that when you are stressed out you become more suspicious or worried about how others view you.

So, under stress, you may perceive that some people are trying to take advantage of you, harm you, think negatively about you, or judge you -- such as "He's fat," "She's ugly," "His comments are stupid." When things go smoothly, one is less likely to feel paranoid or have suspicious thoughts about others.

Part of the concept of "cognitive dysregulation" is "dissociation" which is the experience of slipping away from reality, checking out, spacing out, being in a foggy mental state, not being aware of your surroundings, or feeling outside of your body.

Some people report feeling like they're floating up to the ceiling and looking down on the scene. Dissociation occurs under stress to people with BPD.

Some BPD people may use dissociation to escape when they feel stress. Let's say your wife divorces you or you get fired from your job. One might check out mentally for some time to get away from problems.

The problem with dissociation is that it doesn't solve anything. And one might do something during the dissociation time such as suicide or try a one-night stand, reckless sex, and regret it later.

Psychosis vs. BPD:

BPD is not the same as psychosis -- although some with BPD report feeling crazy, insane, or nuts. However, BPD people can experience short, temporary periods of psychosis at times. The term "Borderline Personality Disorder" does not refer to sitting on the line between sane and insane or psychotic.

Dissociation Types:

Dissociation refers to breaking of connections or associations of self that normally go together. Parts of the self include your body, memories, emotions, identity, thoughts, and even the connection of yourself to reality.

For example, in dissociation a woman who is raped could have a vivid memory of the rape but experience no emotions in connection with that memory.

Dissociation experiences are fairly common among BPD people and do not represent psychosis although it can imply some degree of departure from reality. Dissociation can be a way a person copes with stress to avoid being emotionally overwhelmed.

Next let's consider the forms dissociation can take:

1) Dissociative fugue:

In dissociative fugue, the person disconnects or blanks out the memory of a part of their past. They may disconnect from their identities and travel to a new city and adopt a new identity.

2) Dissociative identity disorder:

Once called "multiple personality disorder" and dramatized in many movies such as *Sybil*, it occurs when a person adopts two or more distinct personalities or personas. Some claim to take on as many as fifteen different identities over time in dissociative identity disorder.

Each personality could represent a different way of dealing with a stressor or problem in their life. Changes from personality to personality can involve voice pitch, vocabulary, dialect, and posture.

A large number of people with this disorder change their handedness from left to right or vice versa as they move from one persona to another. In addition, each personality does not likely have memories of other personalities as the individual changes personas.

3) Dissociative amnesia:

Unlike normal forgetfulness, in dissociative amnesia the person loses big chunks of memory. Usually these memories are traumatic in nature. Some people with dissociative amnesia attempt to conceal this from others.

4) Depersonalization disorder:

When a person feels detached from himself and their experiences for a period of time, this is called depersonalization disorder. They can feel detached from their bodies. Maybe they feel they're viewing themselves through a movie camera -- at times they feel like they're in a dream or a movie.

Process of dissociation:

Dissociative episodes are the way for the mind to escape intolerable situations. For instance, many BPD people report having been abused or experiencing trauma in their lives. The stress of that abuse can lead some into dissociation. Most people with or without BPD experience brief dissociation during highly traumatic experiences.

For example:

Lizzie was sexually abused by her stepfather as a child. When he was molesting her at night, she'd close her eyes and psychologically escape her body in a dissociative condition. She imagines her body is not her own. She wills her mind to go somewhere else -- fly away like a bird.

Lizzie could not cope with the horror of sexual abuse by her stepfather -- so she went into dissociative states in the form of depersonalization in which she psychologically left her body during the assaults. Later in life as an adult she'd go into dissociative states when she was reminded of the abuse or at times of stress.

Paranoid or Delusional:

BPD can commonly involve some paranoid ideation. Paranoia means elevated mistrust, suspicion, and fear. People suffering from paranoia are preoccupied by imagined plots that others may be planning against them.

They could focus on unsupported ideas of betrayal by friends, spouses, or acquaintances despite a lack of evidence. Innocent or unrelated remarks made by others could be read as threatening or maybe ridiculing them -- such as "ideas of reference."

People with BPD tend to have brief paranoid feelings. Paranoia can range on a spectrum from some heightened distrust to full blown delusions of a psychotic nature with no connection to reality. BPD people tend to have paranoid thoughts that have something to do with reality or are temporary.

Here's an example of a BPD person with some paranoid-like distrust:

Rudy, 21, is waiting at home for his girlfriend, Lynn, 19, who is late coming from her college classes. He's called her cell and texts her about 50 times today. She's not answering.

"I bet she's hanging out or screwing her old fraternity boyfriend!" Rudy said to himself. He's getting very angry when finally Lynn walks into his apartment.

"Where the hell have you been? I've been calling you all day," Rudy snarled.

"I'm in no mood for your paranoid shit," Lynn snapped. "I was in science classes and labs all day. They require we shut off our phones. I told you that a dozen times."

"Then you stopped by the fraternity to see Chuckie," Rudy said. "Right? You screwing Chuckie again?"

"Shut up, Rudy," Lynn said. Lynn turned around and headed back out the door. "I'm not putting up with being treated like a criminal. You don't own me!"

"I knew it," Rudy shouted. "Who ya fucking?"

Lynn stomped out of the apartment and slammed the door.

Rudy illustrates over-the-top mistrust of his girlfriend. But his slightly paranoid feelings don't qualify as psychotic delusions. Lynn could have been cheating on him. Although he has no evidence of any betrayal. His BPD has kicked in and he's afraid of abandonment. So his jealous thoughts don't completely depart from reality.

Paranoid Schizophrenia:

Here's an example of paranoid schizophrenia and is distinct from BPD. Harvey has been hospitalized and medicated on a locked psych ward in a state mental hospital. He carries some fake badge and walks around in a trench coat showing his ID -- "I'm with the CIA," Harvey says to hospital staff. He has the delusion that the CIA sends secret messages to him about spies on the hospital staff. He shows a list of spying doctors and nurses to his therapist.

Harvey is out of touch with reality and is psychotic. He's paranoid schizophrenic. Harvey is not a BPD type.

Hallucinations:

Hallucinations involve a person perceiving without input from the environment -- people can hear sounds that are not there, see people who are not present, sense smells, temperature, and tastes from nowhere. These hallucinations happen when a person is awake -- not while they're dreaming.

Normal people, particularly at times of stress, may have very mild hallucinations such as hearing a phone ring while they're in the shower, hearing faint voices or smelling scents with no apparent source. When the phone is checked, there was no missed call, for example.

It is a step up in hallucinations to hear a very distinct sound or seeing sights that come from nowhere. Someone may report hearing voices that are sharp, clear, and present even when nobody is in the room. It is not full-blown psychosis as long as people admit the sounds come from their own heads.

But if a person hears voices loud and clear, notices sights, sounds, and smells nobody else can perceive, and they insist they are real, it can be a serious hallucination on a psychotic level. They may claim alien radio sources are beaming voices into their head.

This type of serious hallucination is very rare in BPD people and if it happens it is very brief and temporary. When this serious type of hallucination is severe and longer-term, the person may have a different type of mental disorder such as schizophrenia.

Hallucinations & Schizophrenia:

Case A:

As an illustration of schizophrenic hallucinations, let's take the case of Brenda. In her dorm room at college she is hearing voices of a demon that has invaded her body:

"Brenda, the devil says you must die!"

Brenda stills the hallucination voices by burning herself with cigarettes. When this doesn't work she takes an overdose of sleeping pills. Her roommate comes in and finds her on the floor unconscious. She's taken to a hospital ER and at first diagnosed as a possible BPD type. But her roommate tells the doctor that she's been complaining of hearing voices, hallucinations. After a psychiatric diagnosis she's found to be schizophrenic and not BPD.

Case B:

Ben, 22, was abused as a child. He's under stress because he's joined the marines and is in basic training. He's stressed-out because he can barely do the physical exercises. He complains to his military supervisor that he's hearing voices in his head but that he knows nobody is talking around him. Ben is not completely detached from reality. He is given a mental health exam and discharged from the marines with a diagnosis of BPD.

BPD, Feeling Crazy & Psychosis:

When people with BPD say they feel crazy, out of it, and dissociating, it does not rise to the level of psychosis. On rare occasions BPD people do temporarily experience psychotic episodes in which they experience hallucinations or delusions for awhile. When this happens they can usually be treated with an anti-psychotic medication. When the episodes stop, the BPD person can be taken off the anti-psychotic meds.

CHAPTER 25: ASSESSING, DIAGNOSING BPD

A clinician doing an intake or initial interview would likely ask questions related to the criteria for BPD if you're suspected of having this disorder. If you have five or more of the nine in the DSM (*Diagnostic Statistical Manual of Mental Disorders*) you have BPD.

Here are the nine criteria:

1) Frantic efforts to avoid real or imagined abandonment

2) A pattern of unstable and intense interpersonal relationships characterized by alternating between extremes of idealization and devaluation

3) Identity disturbance: markedly and persistently unstable self-image or sense of self

4) Impulsivity in at least two areas that are potentially self-damaging (e.G., spending, sex, substance abuse, reckless driving, binge eating)

5) Recurrent suicidal behavior, gestures, or threats, or self-mutilation behavior

6) Affective instability due to a marked reactivity of mood (e.G., intense episodic dysphoria, irritability, or anxiety usually lasting a few hours and only rarely more than a few days)

7) Chronic feelings of emptiness

8) Inappropriate, intense anger or difficulty controlling anger (e.G., frequent displays of temper, constant anger, recurrent physical fights)

9) Transient, stress-related paranoid ideation or severe dissociative symptoms

What can a person who may have BPD expect in a clinical interview with a social worker, psychologist, or psychiatrist? Questions to the client aimed at diagnosing BPD should focus on these areas:

A) Historical patterns of substance abuse (alcohol, mood-altering drugs), gambling, money-spending binges, or sexual promiscuity (indications of impulsive symptoms)

B) Intense beginnings and endings of relationships and cutoff relationships with family members (indicators of unstable relationships)

C) Psychotic-like symptoms, such as depersonalization, derealization, delusions, hallucinations, paranoia, and referential thinking

D) History of sexual, physical or emotional abuse

E) Suicide attempts, self-mutilation, binging and purging, or not eating (indicators of self-destructive behavior)

What do some of these clinical/shrink terms mean?

--Dysphoric: generalized feeling of distress

--Derealization: a sense that one has lost contact with external reality

--Delusions: beliefs maintained despite much evidence or argument to the contrary

--Hallucinations: hearing or seeing things others do not

--Paranoia: having suspicions and beliefs that one is being followed, plotted against, persecuted, etc.

--Referential thinking: mistakenly believing others' actions or external events are specifically related to one's self

--Dissociative or dissociation: an abnormal psychological state in which one's perception of oneself and/or one's environment is altered significantly

--Idealization: the process whereby the patient sees another person as only "good" or "perfect"

--Devaluation (or demonization): the process whereby the patient undervalues the abilities and/or intentions of others

--Impulsive: acting without first thinking about the action

--Compulsive: feeling compelled to act against one's wishes

--Labile affect: marked and rapid mood shifts

--Affect: emotion, feeling; mood

--Hyperphrasia: pathologically excessive talking

--Mild formal thought disorder: disturbances in speech, communication, and/or thinking

--Dissociative ego states: attitudes and emotions that produce anxiety become separated from the rest of the person's personality and function independently

--Neurosis: non-physiological disorder characterized by high levels of anxiety but no impairment in reality testing

--Psychosis: grossly impaired reality testing

--Maladaptive behavior patterns: patterns of behavior likely to produce so much psychic distress that therapy is necessary

What are examples of questions in a clinical interview a clinician might ask somebody who potentially has BPD?

1) Are your relationships stormy or chaotic?

2) Do your emotions or moods change a lot?

3) Have you ever deliberately hurt yourself without meaning to kill yourself?

4) Are you unsure of who you are or what you are really like?

If an individual is a suicide risk, more questions should be asked about that such as:

A) Have you ever thought of hurting yourself?

B) Have you had suicidal thoughts recently?

C) Do you want to commit suicide?

D) Might you do so sometime if things get worse?

E) Do you think about suicide but have no specific plans?

F) Do you sometimes wish you could die?

If the person has active suicide thoughts:

G) When are you planning to commit suicide?

H) How would you do that? What method are you planning to use?

I) Where do you think about killing yourself?

The presence of multiple suicide attempts, especially of low lethality, is likely to indicate the presence of a personality disorder (such as BPD), as compared with an acute clinical disorder.

Patients who have made use of more lethal methods of suicide in the past tend to be more:

1) Serious about actually dying

2) Disappointed that they did not succeed with previous attempts

3) Likely to use highly lethal methods in future attempts

Clients being assessed for possible BPD could be given a self-report and interview instrument or test form such as:

--Borderline Personality Inventory: This instrument is based on a psychodynamic formulation of BPD, while compatible with the DSM criteria. It aims to assess four areas:

1) Identity diffusion

2) Primitive defense mechanisms

3) Reality testing

4) Fear of closeness

--McLean Screening Instrument for Borderline Personality Disorder (MSI-BPD): This is a 10-item screening tool for BPD based on the DSM criteria.

--Objective Behavioral Index: This index assesses treatment response in clients with severe personality disorders. It measures dysfunctional behaviors as well as use of mental health services.

--Personality Assessment Inventory (PAI): This 344-item inventory has four borderline feature subscales: Affective Instability, Identity Problems, Negative Relationships, and Self-Harm.

Interview instruments include:

--Diagnostic Interview for Borderline Personality Disorders: It is based on DSM criteria. It's a one-hour, semi-structured interview focusing on social adaptation, self-destructive impulsiveness, depressive and angry affect, dissociative ego states, and interpersonal relations.

--Structured Clinical Interview for DSM Personality Disorders: It includes questions for 11 different DSM personality disorders.

--Zanarini Rating Scale for Borderline Personality Disorder (ZAN-BPD): This scale was developed to measure change in borderline psychopathology.

Instruments assessing suicide and self-harm include:

--Self-Harm Inventory (SHI): This instrument identifies self-destructive behaviors and is useful as a screening tool for BPD.

--Beck Scale for Suicide Ideation: This scale is a self-administered, 21-item scale assessing frequency and content of suicidal ideation for clinical follow-up.

--Suicide Probability Scale (SPS): This is a 36-item, self-administered scale offering a suicide probability score and detailed information on four subscales: Hopelessness, Suicide Ideation, Negative Self Evaluation, and Hostility.

Psychometric Assessment Tools:

Psychometric instruments that are commonly used for diagnosis also include:

--Minnesota Multiphasic Personality Inventory (MMPI): This instrument consists of 567 statements that the patient rates as either true or false. A profile is constructed based on several scales.

--Wechsler Adult Intelligence Scale -- Revised (WAIS-R): The WAIS-R is an intelligence test developed to:

1) Measure the patient's intellectual potential

2) Obtain clinically relevant information pertaining to the patient's decision-making capacity

3) Determine the ability to process language

4) Assess the functional integrity of the brain

--Rorschach: This test is a "projective" measure of personality. It consists of 10 cards with randomly created inkblots, some in monochrome and some in color. The clinician shows the cards to the client one at a time, records the answers, and later scores them.

--Millon Clinical Multi-Axial Inventory II (MCMI): This self-report questionnaire assesses personality disorders for inpatients and is based on Millon's taxonomy for personality disorders. Taxonomy is a classification system.

CHAPTER 26: HOW IS BPD DIFFERENTIATED FROM OTHER DISORDERS?

The BPD diagnostic category overlaps with other personality disorders, especially affective disorders; narcissistic, antisocial, histrionic, and schizotypal personality disorders; and post-traumatic stress disorder.

Let's consider differentiating BPD from six other disorders:

1) Antisocial Personality Disorder (APD) vs. BPD:

--Those with BPD may perform antisocial acts, but are more likely to feel personal shame or remorse than those with APD.

--People with APD usually regret their actions only because of the consequences to themselves, not others.

--Antisocial acts committed by people with BPD are usually viewed as survival issues, and the individual experiences uncomfortable anxiety as a result. Those with APD usually feel no anxiety about their antisocial behavior.

2) Histrionic Personality Disorder (HPD) vs. BPD:

--Those with HPD have a higher overall functional level, display greater employment and relationship stability, and maintain a more stable self-image.

--Those with HPD do not commit the repeated self-destructive acts typical of BPD.

3) Narcissistic Personality Disorder (NPD) vs. BPD:

--Those with BPD openly express their need for support in interpersonal relationships while those who are narcissistic are more subtle.

--Those with NPD typically deny their many dependency needs and are better able to have consistent and sustained relationships. People with BPD have more extreme affective displays and less stable relationships.

--NPD patients demonstrate grandiosity in contrast to the devalued sense of self evident in people with BPD.

4) Schizotypal Personality Disorder (SPD) vs. BPD:

--The flat affect that often accompanies BPD with depression is usually temporary or state-like (it lifts as the depression lifts). With SPD, flat affect is stable or trait-like.

--Clinicians view the psychotic symptoms present in those with SPD to be more trait-like, while similar symptoms among those with BPD are more transient, stress-related, or state-like.

--Those with BPD have significantly higher rates of depression as well as substance abuse compared to those with SPD.

5) Affective Disturbance (Depression, Dysthymia, Bipolar Disorder) vs. BPD:

--Some researchers argue that BPD is a part of the affective disturbance spectrum. Others highlight the overlap between BPD and affective disturbance.

--People who have affective instability, but who function well with minimal support and intervention, likely suffer from an affective disorder and would not meet BPD criteria.

6) Post-Traumatic Stress Disorder (PTSD) vs. BPD:

--Those with BPD have often experienced significant trauma; however, they do not as a matter of course, experience PTSD symptoms (e.G., hypervigilance, exaggerated startle response, flashbacks, intrusive recollections, or efforts to avoid trauma-related thoughts and feelings).

--The dissociative symptoms associated with PTSD are a direct result of trauma-related stimuli rather than general stress-related dissociative symptoms seen with BPD.

--Many people with BPD also suffer from PTSD.

CHAPTER 27: INDIVIDUAL & GROUP PSYCHOTHERAPY & BPD

There are various individual & group psychotherapeutic approaches to treating BPD which include:

1) Psychodynamic Approach: This approach seeks to produce broad-based character change in which patients gain control of their overwhelming emotions. This control process (also referred to as ego mastery) allows the patients the capacity to form stable relationships and maintain an integrated sense of self.

2) Psychoanalytic Approach: Psychoanalytic theorists view BPD as developmental in nature. These theorists believe that people with BPD experienced early trauma that has frustrated or inhibited normal developmental growth. This trauma has kept the person at a "primitive" (or childlike) level of psychic functioning.

3) Interpersonal Psychotherapy (IPT): This approach is based on the theory of personality developed by H.S. Sullivan. This theory defines personality as a relatively enduring pattern of recurrent interpersonal situations.

IPT assumes that interpersonal interactions shape current behavior. Consequently, disordered behavior or communications are a result of disordered interpersonal relations.

4) Cognitive Therapy: This theory assumes that dysfunction stems from maladaptive schemas. These maladaptive schemas result in biased judgments that lead patients to consistently rationalize their own dysfunctional behavior and to be unable to test their interpretations against reality.

For example, this approach views people with BPD as holding unrealistic expectations regarding current interpersonal relationships based on rigid beliefs about relationships with early primary caregivers.

5) Dialectical Behavior Therapy (DBT): These theorists stress the relationship between biological and environmental forces. For example, this theory sees the person with BPD as biologically predisposed to being vulnerable to emotional extremes while being influenced by an emotionally invalidating environment.

6) Cognitive Analytic Therapy: This is a relatively new therapy that helps patients identify and alter reciprocal relationship roles learned through early childhood experiences.

7) Relapse Prevention: The relapse prevention model is a social learning model that does not specifically address people with BPD. However, it is a theoretical model for treating people who struggle with addictions.

Since people with BPD often have one or more addictions or compulsive behaviors based on immediate gratification, the components of relapse prevention represent important considerations for treatment.

8) Group Psychotherapy: Group psychotherapy is the treatment of choice for some BPD therapists. It offers multiple interpersonal relationships in a controlled group setting. Since unstable interpersonal relationships is an important symptom of BPD, improving interpersonal relationship skills in group therapy can be very helpful.

Treatment strategies:

1) Reality testing: Feedback from group members from their peers can be more credible to BPD people than an authority figure like a therapist/clinician. So feedback can help reduce interpersonal distortions, get BPD clients to face a difficult reality, and lessen the expression of intense primitive fears and needs.

2) Viewing how the patient relates to others: In the group, patients tend to recreate or act-out family relationships and interpersonal patterns outside the group. So clinicians are shown the interpersonal style or problems group members have. This can lead to a focus for possible healthy changes.

3) Reducing transference reactions: The transference process is speeded up and reduced in group therapy because there are more people providing reality testing and the more people receive the transference reactions. Transference reactions are a very rich source of material which can uncover dysfunctional thoughts and assumptions.

Transference, on a cognitive level, refers to clients reacting to the clinician/therapist based on generalized beliefs and expectations they have about relationships, rather than on how the therapist behaves as an individual. As transference conflicts emerge, the group therapist can clarify the client's misunderstandings or misconceptions and resolve the issue.

An effective group leader or therapist should be alert and use countertransference signals from BPD group members. Countertransference refers to clinicians' emotions that are triggered by something the patients said or did.

4) Healing: Group therapy is an opportunity for the BPD client to heal in the context of being respected, taken seriously, and guided in a healthy direction by the group and therapist.

5) Identification: BPD people can internalize the ways and skills the therapist shows in dealing with interpersonal relations within the group. Additionally, the patient can internalize the positive coping skills of other group members.

Identification is the process whereby the patient internalizes behavior aspects of important others.

6) Stimulation: More withdrawn or schizoid-like BPD people can get benefits from the stimulation of group interaction.

7) Peer pressure: Peer pressure can help set limits for members with poor control and impulsive behaviors. Peer pressure is one of the keys to twelve-step programs such as A.A., N.A., etc.

8) Changing behavior: Group therapy provides BPD people with a lab to improve their intimacy skills -- improve interpersonal communication. Discussion can include self-harm and self-mutiliation or other negative tendencies BPD people use which distances others, lessens intimacy

communication, and group therapy is then an avenue leading to healthy outcomes.

9) Other curative factors: Both universality and existential factors can help make group therapy effective for BPD patients. Universality is the sense of not being alone in one's struggles. Existential factors refers to social aloneness, self-responsibility, and coming to terms with mortality.

CHAPTER 28: NEUROBIOLOGICAL INDICATIONS FOR BPD

In the BPD literature, four prominent clusters of BPD symptoms emerge with different underlying neurochemical systems:

1) Affective instability: In theory, these symptoms are related to the brain's adrenergic and cholinergic systems.

Symptoms include: labile affect, irritability such as intense outbursts of anger, mood instability, low mood or dysphoria, and stress-related decompensation.

Term definitions:

A) Adrenergic -- a neuronal pathway in the adrenal gland that produces adrenaline (also known as epinephrine)

B) Cholinergic -- neurons and neural pathways that release the neurotransmitter, acetylcholine, which is involved in stimulating sweat glands and fibers to skeletal muscles

C) Decompensation -- a failure of one's defense mechanisms leading to an exacerbation of BPD symptoms

2) Depression: This cluster of symptoms is also related to abnormalities in the brain's adrenergic and cholinergic systems.

Symptoms include: depressed mood, loss of interest in life's activities, insomnia or hypersomnia, poor attention and concentration, and recurrent suicidal ideation.

3) Transient psychoticism: Abnormalities in central dopaminergic systems may be the basis of temporary psychotic experiences. The neurotransmitter dopamine appears to impact motor control systems, limbic systems, and schizophrenia.

Symptoms of transitory, stress-related psychotic conditions include: referential thinking, derealization or depersonalization, paranoia, distortion of reality, and magical thinking.

Term definitions:

A) Dopaminergic -- neural pathways in which the neurotransmitter dopamine (which appears to inhibit motor control systems and limbic activity) is involved

B) Neurotransmitter -- chemical agents that affect behavior, mood, and feelings

C) Limbic -- associated with autonomic functions and certain aspects of emotions and behavior

4) Impulsive aggressive behavior: Abnormalities in central nervous system serotonergic functioning appear to underlie impulsive aggressive behaviors, particularly suicide attempts.

Serotonergic refers to neurons and neural pathways that release the neurotransmitter serotonin.

CHAPTER 29: MEDICATIONS TO TREAT BPD

Medication effectiveness varies with BPD patients. Drugs mostly address three main symptom clusters:

1) Impulsive/aggressive behavioral dyscontrol

2) Affective instability

3) Cognitive/perceptual disturbances

Prescribed drugs with some positive outcomes include:

A) Divalproex sodium for irritability, anger, and impulsive aggression

B) Fluvoxamine for affective instability (rapid mood shifts)

C) Olanzapine for all three symptom groups (affective, cognitive/perceptual, impulsive/aggressive

D) Topiramate for anger

E) E-EPA (omega 3 fatty acid) for aggression and depressive symptoms

Medications have been found to be most effective for acute BPD symptoms, less useful for maintenance. These medications have been used to treat BPD symptoms:

--Selective Serotonin Reuptake Inhibitors (SSRIs)

--Selective Serotonin Norepinephrine Reuptake Inhibitors (SSNRIs)

--A Norepinephrine Reuptake Inhibitor (NRI)

--Antipsychotic Medications (Atypical and Typical)

--Anticonvulsants

--An Opiate Antagonist

--An Antimanic Agent

--Benzodiazepines

--An Omega 3 Fatty Acid

--An Antihypertensive Agent

Due to the suicide potential of those with BPD, the prescribing physician or psychiatrist must carefully consider medication lethality and the number of pills given in a single prescription.

Classes of medications used to treat BPD:

Neuroleptics and atypical antipsychotic agents are the medication groups that have been studied most for the treatment of BPD.

Neuroleptics were the first generation of drugs to treat psychotic disorders and mostly included:

--chlopromazine (Thorazine)

--trifluoperazine (Stelazine)

--haloperidol (Haldol)

--thiothixene (Navane)

Atypical antipsychotics are the second generation of medications to treat psychotic disorders including:

--clozaphine (Clozaril)

--olanzapine (Zyprexa)

--risperidone (Risperdal)

--quetiapine (Seroquel)

--ziprasidone (Geodon)

--aripiprazole (Abilify)

Medications Studied and Used in the Treatment of Borderline Personality Disorder:

1) Antipsychotics:

1.1) Drug class: Antipsychotics -- neuroleptics

Medications: thiothixene (Navane), haloperidol (Haldol), trifluoperazine (Stelazine), flupenthixol

Symptoms improved by one or more medications in the class of neuroleptics: anxiety, obsessive-compulsivity, depression, suicide attempts, hostility, self-injury/assaultiveness, illusions, paranoid thinking, psychoticism, poor general functioning

1.2) Drug class: Antipsychotics -- Atypical

Medications: olanzapine (Zyprexa), risperidone (Risperdal), clozapine (Clozaril)

Symptoms improved by one or more medications in the class of Atypical: anxiety, anger/hostility, paranoid thinking, self-injury, impulsive aggression, interpersonal

2) Antidepressants:

2.1) Drug class: Antidepressants -- SSRIs (selective serotonin reuptake inhibitors) and related antidepressants

Medications: fluoxetine (Prozac), fluvoxamine (Luvox), sertraline (Zoloft), venlafaxine (Effexor)

Symptoms improved by one or more medications in the class of SSRIs: anxiety, depression, mood swings, impulsivity, anger/hostility, self-injury, impulsive aggression, poor general functioning

2.2) Drug class: MAOIs (monoamine oxidase inhibitors) -- phenelzine (Nardil)

Medications: phenelzine (Nardil)

Symptoms improved by one or more medications in the class of MAOIs: depression, anger/hostility, mood swings, rejection sensitivity, impulsivity

2.3) Drug class: other antidepressants

Medications: bupropion (Wellbutrin)

3) Mood Stabilizers (drug class)

Medications: divalproex (Depakote), lamotrigine (Lamictal), carbamazepine (Tegretol), lithium

Symptoms improved by one or more medications in the class of mood stabilizers: unstable mood, anxiety, depression, anger, irritability, impulsivity, aggression, suicidality, poor general functioning

4) Nutriceutical Agents (drug class)

Medications: Omega 3 fatty acids

Symtoms: aggression, depression

CHAPTER 30: ST -- NEW BPD PSYCHOTHERAPY

This chapter is to introduce a new therapy model for BPD clients which can be used by clinicians (psychologists, social workers, psychiatrists) or therapists: ST -- Spiritual Therapy.

ST is based on the spiritual program used in twelve-step programs such as A.A., Alcoholics Anonymous. Many Borderline Personality Disorder people have impulsivity behaviors such as substance abuse (alcohol, drugs), spending, sex, eating disorders, gambling, etc. There are twelve-step programs for these addictions. So many BPD people should be familiar with twelve-step programs.

If, for example, a BPD person is an active alcoholic or drug addict, he/she will need to go to a twelve-step program before going to psychotherapy. Therapy will not work if BPD people are lost in their addictions.

I have found that twelve-step programs work better than most psychotherapy methods anyway. I have known people with chronic mental disorders including schizophrenia who only became healthy and functional after working a twelve-step program such as A.A. Some had been in mental hospitals or institutions for years and had made no progress until they worked a twelve-step program.

My ST -- Spiritual Therapy -- theoretical model follows the basics of the twelve-step programs. It can be used in individual or group therapy. The therapist or client can just replace the word "alcohol" or "drugs" in the A.A. or N.A. (Narcotics Anonymous) literature, insert BPD, and apply the suggestions.

For example, in the basic *Alcoholics Anonymous* book, in Chapter 5, "How It Works," is a list of the twelve steps. Take Step One and insert "BPD" in place of "alcohol" and Step One becomes:

1. We admitted we were powerless over BPD (Borderline Personality Disorder) that our lives had become unmanageable.

The other step mentioning alcoholics is Step Twelve. So insert BPD in Step Twelve:

12. Having had a spiritual awakening as the result of these steps, we tried to carry this message to BPDs

(Borderline Personality Disordered), and to practice these principles in all our affairs.

As a clinical psychologist I was trained in a number of psychotherapy methods and used a number of therapy techniques with clients. But over the years I've found that the twelve-step program works better than traditional psychotherapy.

So I am advocating using the twelve-step model in individual and group therapy. I've found that it works. I know that some clinicians, psychologists, psychiatrists reading this will panic at the thought of a spiritual approach or praying to God.

For example, let's say a BPD client has a problem with resentments. The usual suggestion in twelve-step programs is to pray for the person one has a resentment against. While it is normally suggested that a person do the prayers for two weeks, I've found that one or two days is often enough.

I know the average clinician who, like me, received many years of scientific method training, will be possibly shocked by the idea of praying to God over a resentment problem, for instance. It doesn't sound scientific.

My graduate school professors lectured me on scientific experimental designs, statistics, and psychotherapy methods verified by rigorous scientific research. How could a psychologist, a doctor, psychiatrist, or social worker possibly pray to God or tell clients to pray to God to solve a problem?

I'm just advocating the twelve-step spiritual program because it works. For example, I've tried various psychotherapy methods with people with resentments or anger issues. And some of the therapy methods work a little bit.

But if every time a client gets angry, resentful, or relives old hurts and hates, is it practical to run to his shrink? Or step-up his psych medications? If the doctor/clinician advises his client to pray to God to let go of anger, patients will make more progress between therapy sessions.

Some of the psychotherapy approaches work to make people feel better. The problem is that they don't get any better. But when I had clients, including myself, just pray for the best for those we have resentments against, the resentment is soon lifted. I've found that the resentment, anger, negative feeling often is reversed in moments with prayer to a higher power or God.

If the resentment returns the next day, continued prayer usually eliminates resentments within a week or two. The key is to pray for the best for the person we are mad at -- pray that they get what they want. It's counter-intuitive and it works.

There are other methods from the twelve-step programs which can help center clients. For instance, as one progresses through the steps, one does a personal inventory at Step Four of resentments.

From "How It Works" in the A.A. book:

"Resentment is the "number one" offender. It destroys more BPD people than anything else. From it stem all forms of spiritual disease, for we have been not only mentally and physically ill, we have been spiritually sick..."

Again, I'm replacing the word "alcoholic" with BPD.

The Fourth Step of the twelve-step programs is aimed at resentments and involves doing an inventory. There is an example of the inventory format in "How It Works" in the A.A. book:

1) I'm resentful at: Mr. Brown

1.1) The cause: His attention to my wife.

1.2) Affects my: Sex relations, Self-esteem (fear).

2) I'm resentful at: My employer

2.1) The cause: Unreasonable, unjust, overbearing. Threatens to fire me for drinking and padding my expense account.

2.2) Affects my: Self-esteem (fear), security.

BPD people, between ST individual or group therapy, can attend twelve-step meetings that are appropriate to any addictions they have. If they don't have a particular addiction, the BPD individual can attend Al-Anon which is another twelve-step program. Al-Anon is a fellowship of relatives and friends of alcoholics and addicts who share their experience, strength, and hope just like other twelve-step programs.

Participants in the ST individual or group sessions can do the steps as part of their homework or do it while attending a twelve-step program. The format for ST is less formal than the twelve-step meeting rituals.

One effective homework assignment for clients is to write a gratitude list, a "did well" list, and a list of resentments on a daily basis. This along with meditation and prayer will help center clients emotionally.

However, there are a number of positive benefits in following the general twelve-step approach. ST clients such as BPD people follow the structure of sharing about themselves only. There is no cross-talk or advice giving to other therapy group members. This means that angry confrontations, which could be transference from other group members, is not allowed.

People can show their emotions in ST, of course, but in the context of sharing about themselves -- not projecting it onto other group members. If clients in ST appear to recreate relationship patterns in the group, the ST clinician/therapist can provide some feedback. But this should be done in a respectful, kind way -- not in a harsh, confrontational approach.

ST, Spiritual Therapy, is not a religious program. But it is a good idea to at least say the twelve-step Serenity Prayer at the end of the ST individual or group session. Here's the Serenity Prayer:

God grant us the serenity to accept the things we cannot change, Courage to change the things we can. And wisdom to know the difference.

I understand some hardcore, scientific clinicians will react against ST as being a spiritual psychotherapy. At one point, I was skeptical of the twelve-step programs.

But over the years I've come to realize that the twelve-step spiritual programs are very effective in treating not only addictions but mental disorders in general. For more details on ST, read the basic A.A. book for the basic spiritual approach.

Practical, inexpensive: Besides the fact that therapy does not work on active addictions (alcohol, drugs, spending, gambling, eating disorders, etc.), so BPD people should be going to their local twelve-step program, professionally led group or individual therapy can be very expensive per hour.

Twelve-step programs are free and only ask for 1 or 2 dollars in a contribution for expenses. Many private rehabs charge $50,000 to $100,000 for a 30-day program. While ST for BPD people would be comparable to other private therapy, it would better fit with ongoing twelve-step programs BPD people should be attending.

If a BPD person is short of cash, they could see a psychiatrist or physician for appropriate medication, if needed, and combine that with regular twelve-step attendance.

Twelve-step program fellowship:

Between psychotherapy sessions, clients can get a sponsor in the twelve-step program or get phone numbers of other participants and call them with problems. Whether the patient is in a twelve-step program aimed at addictions or in Al-Anon, the program for family or friends of addicts, alcoholics, or others (eating disorders -- overeaters anonymous, etc.), he/she can find new friends who will identify with their issues.

Twelve-step literature:

Another source of help between psychotherapy sessions is the twelve-step literature available. Besides the basic "Big Book" of A.A., there are many other twelve-step books. For example, in "Daily Reflections" there are one-page messages for each day of the year.

In the index of "Daily Reflections", almost any problem or concern is covered including: anger, ego deflation, emotional sobriety, fear, forgiveness, grandiosity, higher power, humility, inferiority (feelings of), loneliness, meditation, obsession, pain (emotional), prayer, the promises, resentments, self-awareness, self-will, tolerance, willingness. One can turn to the page on the particular topic and get help.

For example, in the basic A.A. book (the "Big Book") in Chapter 6, pp. 86-87 have some helpful passages which should be read on a daily basis -- here are some excerpts:

"...When we retire at night, we constructively review our day. Were we resentful, selfish, dishonest, or afraid? Do we owe an apology? Have we kept something to ourselves which should be discussed with another person at once? Were we kind and loving toward all? What could we have done better?"

"Were we thinking of ourselves most of the time? Or were we thinking of what we could do for others... But we must be careful not to drift into worry, remorse or morbid reflection, for that would diminish our usefulness to others. After making our review, we ask God's forgiveness and inquire what corrective measures should be taken..."

"On awakening let us think about the twenty-four hours ahead. We consider our plans for the day. Before we begin, we ask God to direct our thinking, especially asking that it be diverted from self-pity, dishonest or self-seeking motives..."

"In thinking about our day we may face indecision. We may not be able to determine which course to take. Here we ask God for inspiration, an intuitive thought or a decision. We relax and take it easy. We don't struggle."

"We are often surprised how the right answers come after we have tried this for a while. What used to be the hunch or the occasional inspiration gradually becomes a working part of the mind. Being still inexperienced and having just made conscious contact with God, it is not probable that we are going to be inspired at all times."

"We might pay for this presumption in all sorts of absurd actions and ideas. Nevertheless, we find that our thinking will, as time passes, be more and more on the plane of inspiration. We come to rely upon it."

"We usually conclude the period of meditation with a prayer that we be shown all through the day what our next step is to be, that we be given whatever we need to take care of such problems. We ask especially for freedom from self-will, and are careful to make no requests for ourselves only."

"We may ask for ourselves, however, if others will be helped. We are careful never to pray for our own selfish ends. Many of us have wasted a lot of time doing that and it doesn't work. You can easily see why..."

There is a reason millions of people have been helped with addictions, various mental disorders, and various reality problems by attending and working twelve-step spiritual programs. It works. And that's why I've developed ST -- Spiritual Therapy following the twelve-step model in individual and group therapy.

CHAPTER 31: INTERSELF TEST & SEVEN-SELVES PROFILE

While I was completing my Ph.D. in psychology at The New School for Social Research, Graduate Faculty, I created and developed a "Seven Selves" theory of personality and self-concept, an assessment instrument or Interself Test to measure personality and self-concept, and a profile format in seven parts or "selves" divided into three stages (Copyright 1979, 2013 by Paul Dawson).

I've used this Interself Test and Seven Selves Profile as a clinician/psychologist in private practice and institutions (mental hospital, prisons, clinics). There are two ways to complete the Seven-Selves profile:

1) The quick way -- just ask the client where he thinks he'd score on each of the seven parts, and which stage he'd expect to fit.

2) Take my 100-item Interself Test, score it, and it breaks down the Seven Selves or parts across three stages (Growth, Transition, or Conflict).

I came up with an acronym (D-O-M-A-I-N-S) using the first letter of each of the Seven Selves. The seven parts or Seven Selves of personality & self-concept in my theory are:

1) Dynamic Self: energy, self-assertion, motivation.

2) Objective Self: social image, reputation, what others think of you.

3) Mirror Self: interpersonal, how you get along with others, what you think they think of you.

4) Actual Self: the way I am, my present reality, problem-solving ability.

5) Ideal Self: the way I would like to be, conscience, future goals.

6) Naive Self: unconscious habits and emotions.

7) Social Self: conscious feelings and sense of identity.

This is my original Seven-Selves theory of personality and self-concept in the context of a therapy workshop:

All kinds of new options in psychotherapy are opening up these days. This proliferation also has created some confusion and frustration. People are increasingly aware of personal problems and of the availability of a great range of psychological help systems. But to find one's way around the various theories and choose one which is relevant can be bewildering.

The layperson can help himself. But people are more complicated than they give themselves credit (or blame) for. This is shown in the frequent difficulty of predicting oneself. People tend not to take cognizance of *all* of themselves. There is "more" to them than they realize.

"How can I say what I really mean? How can I come across to the people who matter to me -- lover, friend, offspring, parent, boss, associate -- to make myself understood and accepted? How can I really accomplish the things I truly want to do?"

To meet any of these questions which all of us put to ourselves, we first need to know ourselves: our *whole* selves, *all* of our "selves."

This new self-concept is embedded in the classical psychology of which all current theories are heirs. It draws upon and synthesizes the vital contributions of psychologists holding distinctive self-concepts.

Added to this integration is the particular innovative factor of the *Dynamic Self*, representing a force in the personality I came to regard as pivotal -- motivation.

William James, perhaps America's greatest psychologist, derived a theory of self embodying two basic entities: the self-as-known (*the empirical Me*) and the self-as-knower (the *Ego* or I). Pertinent to the Seven-Selves theory is James' "social" aspect of the *empirical Me*, which multiplies with each recognition received from others.

The fluid aspect of the social-self and mirror-self in the Seven-Selves therapy program is analogous to James' "social" aspect of the *empirical Me concept.*

Sigmund Freud initiated a tripartite theory of id, super-ego, and ego. Freud's ego-concept is parallel to the self-concept of the Seven-Selves system in terms of an *awareness*. Much of Freud's theory, of course, was based on prescientific and mythological, empirically untestable, instinct-formulations from the nineteenth century.

But Freud's impact is rendered in my "Naive Self" viewpoint of the unconscious. Self-image is not a focus in Freudian theory. Self-image is vital in Seven-Selves.

Kurt Lewin's concept of "life-space" relates to self-concept in that he is talking about psychological space known in one's own personal experience. Lewin's life-space parallels my "Objective-Self", and vivifies the need for my Dynamic-Self innovation.

George Mead, the sociologist, stressed self-awareness as a major influence on perceptions and behaviors. My "Mirror-Self" is directly derived from early twentieth-century sociologist theory. For instance, Daniel Kulp, an educational sociologist summarizing earlier discoveries, wrote of *five* selves.

I have taken the five names for various selves Kulp discusses (Objective, Mirror, Ideal, Naive, Social) and to these have added "Dynamic." Also added is the Actual-Self from Cattell's theory of self. Kulp's use of *mirror* was based on Cooley's "looking-glass self" concept.

However, there is a degree of difference between my definition of the six selves Kulp and Cattell reveal. The present theory of seven personalities or parts considers the conscious and unconscious to be directly linked in continuous interaction.

Counter-opposed to this formulation is Carl Rogers' self-concept approach, which asserts a discontinuity between conscious and unconscious. But Rogers likewise perceives the importance of positive self-feelings in awareness for productive behavior.

Cattell (as per the Seven-Selves theory) segments the self into such aspects as those concerning awareness and sentiment, and names an actual-self and an ideal-self. These latter two are generally parallel in significance to the Seven-Selves Actual/Ideal distinction.

Allport theorized that self was both object and process which is in alignment with the present theory. His concept of the functions of the self coincidentally includes seven features which he discusses developmentally in terms of childhood-growth stages. In Allport's view, by the end of adolescence, an individual has acquired the seven aspects of self.

Seven-Selves therapy theory is based on four views of consciousness derived from self and influenced by communication theory:

1) Selves *known to the individual and others*:

The first quadrant comprises the Social Self and the Dynamic Self. Dynamic Self, the particular innovation, is the self of motivation, drive, assertion, and aggressiveness. For example, if you have intense energy and desire, you can accomplish a specific goal in life.

2) The self *only others know* is the Objective Self -- "as others see you."

3) Selves that *only you know*: Actual Self, Mirror Self, Ideal Self. The definition of the Actual Self is "the way I am now" -- the real self you know from your experience. The Interself Test measures this key Actual-Self construct.

4) The self nobody knows -- Naive Self.

As a helpful acronym one can use D-O-M-A-I-N-S, a word with the first letter of each of the Seven Selves -- the "domains" of your personality.

GOALS -- this system can offer you these specifics to:

1) Strengthen communication and relationships with others.

2) Life your unconscious attitudes into awareness.

3) Enrich your dream interpretation skill.

METHODS: Seven-Selves therapy is designed for the specific self in question. The Seven-Selves Interself Test and therapy are relevant to individuals at every phase of the life cycle, to adults and children alike.

The clinical/educational context of the therapy is aimed at adults, families, children and/or educators, counselors/therapists working with children, business people, and women.

Here is a copy of the INTERSELF TEST and the scoring key. If any clinicians want to research it further, please contact me for permission (Email: dawsonmalibu@gmail.Com):

INTERSELF TEST

Copyright (c) 1979, 2013 by Paul Dawson

All Rights Reserved

INSTRUCTIONS: Write-in one of the following numbers that best answers each question/item:

0 = Definite No

2 = Usually No

4 = Unsure/Maybe

6 = Usually Yes

8 = Definite Yes

1) I'd consider it tactful to laugh at a joke I didn't get.

2) I've been known to name-drop (use well-known names to impress).

3) I'm not always up on major current news.

4) I always act myself, regardless of where I am.

5) I often feel, "I should have handled that differently."

6) When you come down to it, I couldn't hurt a fly.

7) Do you feel that where you really shine is on the phone?

8) I may listen to a story about a mutual acquaintance.

9) Walking into a roomful of people is an interesting experience.

10) I may "go along" to put the other person at ease.

11) Do you feel that certain words or acts of yours determined everything?

12) It could be said of me that I'm honest to a fault.

13) Do you feel you're not getting anywhere?

14) If I got into a movie without paying, I couldn't enjoy the show.

15) I avoid controversial subjects.

16) Books I read, shows I watch, places I visit, are picked mostly by what others tell me.

17) I don't flaunt my education or position.

18) Do you ever plan retaliation?

19) Gossip disgusts me.

20) I enjoy hearing my title (status, accreditation) mentioned.

21) After being abused, do you "put down" the guilty one?

22) Does a crank call seem part of a sinister campaign?

23) If a person insults me, I write a steaming letter.

24) My style, diction, etc., is different in formal circumstances.

25) Do you often have symptoms that worry you?

26) Do you often prefer a pet to people?

27) When phone or doorbell rings, do you tend to feel apprehension?

28) Do you consider yourself lucky?

29) Morning is my big time of day.

30) Colors, scenery, sightseeing turn me on.

31) Do you find it next to impossible to write letters of application?

32) Do you frequently relive particular past events?

33) I'm unimpressed by important contacts.

34) I may express political opinions I can't really back up.

35) I may blame mail, trains, "out of town" for late action.

36) I feel exploited, but don't dare "rock the boat".

37) I enjoy picking out what I'm going to wear.

38) Sometimes I feel like smashing someone.

39) I might relate events as more creditably to myself.

40) Can you "get mad all over again just thinking about it"?

41) Is your sleep often disturbed?

42) I make engagements I don't want to keep when the time comes.

43) Sometimes when I wake up I feel I can't face the day.

44) Do you often feel "Everything I really wanted to say just went out of my head"?

45) I might embroider or exaggerate an anecdote a bit.

46) Sometimes I'd hate for anyone to be able to read my mind.

47) When treated badly, do you get on the phone to a friend?

48) As a love relationship peaks, do you shy away or consult others?

49) Do you "sleep on it" when someone close hurts you?

50) Is it true that I don't have a mean bone in my body?

51) Do you long to meet up with people from out of your past?

52) I may justify postponement of chores as needing time to think on it.

53) Do you work a lot at trying to get the past into focus?

54) I may do things in dreams that shock me when I wake up.

55) If a cabdriver or waiter is rude, does it ruin your whole evening?

56) I may indicate comprehension of a foreign or legal phrase unfamiliar to me.

57) Is much of your thinking given over to daydreaming?

58) When I get a harmless urge, I act on it.

59) I call a lawyer when at odds with others.

60) Do you praise insincerity, to maintain "good feeling"?

61) Are you ambitious?

62) When at odds with next-of-kin, I discuss it with outsiders.

63) Do you have detailed fantasies of romantic and material success?

64) Are you often convinced you've lost ten dollars (or other money)?

65) People like me for what I am.

66) Anticipation seizes me when the phone rings.

67) I want to prolong the tension when my social life gets exciting.

68) Talking it over with everyone helps when I get walked on.

69) Do you push to a commitment in a romance?

70) Do you feel you receive too few or perfunctory Christmas cards?

71) I tend to feel, "Everybody's got somebody, except me."

72) Do you resent successful people as "pushy", or "just out for themselves""

73) I feel I don't know what to do in bed.

74) Do you wish you could be made love to without "doing" anything?

75) Are you most aware of loving a person when threatened with his (her) loss?

76) Does a knock at the door annoy you?

77) Theater and TV programs are picked mostly by relevance to my main pursuits.

78) Do you frequently feel "I'm not much fun to be with"?

79) Is it awkward for you to wind up a conversation?

80) My references and record show my strengths best.

81) Writing letters of complaint or protest is easy for me.

82) People who acknowledge others' small good deeds are doing butter-ups, in my opinion.

83) Do you frequently feel "Something is wrong with me I'd rather not know"?

84) My selection of recreational activities is purely by emotional whim.

85) Do you often think or say, "I couldn't stand it" or "I'd never get over it"?

86) Condolence letters are hard for me to get around to writing.

87) I make a strong impression in interviews.

88) When I get caught in a big crowd, I panic or get intensely anxious.

89) If something I made isn't perfect, I won't present it to others.

90) I work hard night and day toward my long-term goals.

91) I usually feel great after a social occasion.

92) Forces from my past frustrate my chance of success.

93) I worry about how I'll "do" sexually.

94) My moods "swing" too sharply.

95) I feel self-conscious about going to a movie or event without a companion.

96) I must tell lies to keep my relationships with people smooth.

97) Do you see lack of accomplishment as your biggest problem?

98) I have enough energy to accomplish what I want.

99) I got some good points from my parents.

100) Do you wish you were popular like some other people?

Examiner/clinician or client should list the question/item number next to any comments or summarize special concerns.

INTERSELF ANSWER KEY -- REVEALS SEVEN-SELVES PROFILE:

1) DYNAMIC-SELF:

Dynamic-Self score is a total of 22 less incorrect items.

Dynamic-Self stages:

1.1) Growth stage: 16-22 (some work needed)

1.2) Transition stage: 11-15 (moderate degree work needed)

1.3) Conflict stage: 0-10 (intensive work needed)

Dynamic-Self items/questions (correct answers):

6) 0 or 2

11) 0 or 2

13) 0 or 2

18) 6 or 8

21) 6 or 8

29) 6 or 8

30) 6 or 8

31) 0 or 2

32) 0 or 2

35) 0 or 2

36) 0 or 2

38) 6 or 8

57) 0 or 2

58) 6 or 8

61) 6 or 8

74) 0 or 2

81) 6 or 8

86) 0 or 2

90) 6 or 8

92) 0 or 2

97) 0 or 2

98) 0 or 2

2) OBJECTIVE-SELF:

Objective-Self score is to be estimated:

2.1) Growth stage (some work needed)

2.2) Transition stage (moderate degree work needed)

2.3) Conflict stage (intensive work needed)

3) MIRROR-SELF:

Mirror-Self score is a total of 40 less incorrect items/questions.

Mirror-Self stages:

3.1) Growth stage: 28-40 (some work needed)

3.2) Transition stage: 21-27 (moderate degree work needed)

3.3) Conflict stage: 0-20 (intensive work needed)

Mirror-Self items/questions (correct answers):

1) 0 or 2

2) 6 or 8

3) 6 or 8

4) 0 or 2

7) 0 or 2

8) 6 or 8

10) 0 or 2

12) 0 or 2

14) 0 or 2

15) 0 or 2

16) 0 or 2

17) 0 or 2

19) 0 or 2

20) 6 or 8

26) 0 or 2

33) 0 or 2

34) 6 or 8

39) 6 or 8

45) 6 or 8

46) 6 or 8

48) 0 or 2

50) 0 or 2

52) 0 or 2

56) 0 or 2

59) 0 or 2

60) 0 or 2

62) 0 or 2

65) 6 or 8

67) 0 or 2

69) 6 or 8

70) 0 or 2

71) 0 or 2

73) 0 or 2

78) 0 or 2

79) 0 or 2

80) 0 or 2

87) 6 or 8

96) 0 or 2

99) 6 or 8

100) 6 or 8

4) ACTUAL-SELF:

Actual-Self score is a total 100 less total number incorrect (mark test items "as I am now").

4.1) Growth stage: 70+ (some work needed)

4.2) Transition stage: 50-69 (moderate degree work needed)

4.3) Conflict: 0-49 (intensive work needed)

5) IDEAL-SELF:

Ideal-Self score is 100 less the total number of incorrect items. Either re-take test marking items "as I would like to be/future goals" or simply check estimated stage.

5.1) Growth stage: 85 or more or estimate (some work needed)

5.2) Transition stage: 70-84 or estimate (moderate degree work needed)

5.3) Conflict stage: 0-69 or estimate (intensive work needed)

6) NAIVE-SELF:

Naive-Self score is the total number wrong.

6.1) Growth stage: 0-30 (some work needed)

6.2) Transition stage: 31-50 (moderate degree work needed)

6.3) Conflict stage: 51-100 (intensive work needed)

I'd be interested to get the results of systematic research showing the pattern of the Seven-Selves profile for Borderline Personality Disorder people. If any professional, doctoral level psychologist or psychiatrists want to use my INTERSELF TEST & SEVEN-SELVES profile in research, please request permission and submit credentials. My email is: dawsonmalibu@gmail.com.

REFERENCES:

Conversations with Marilyn by W.J. Weatherby

Borderline Personality Disorder by John M. Grohol

The Ultimate Marilyn by Ernest W. Cunningham

Heroes & Heroines by Tami D. Cowden, Caro LaFever, Sue Viders

And Never Let Her Go by Ann Rule

Borderline Personality Disorder by Melanie Dean

Serial Killers by Peter Vronsky

Post-Traumatic Stress Disorder for Dummies by Mark Goulston

Girl, Interrupted by Susanna Kaysen

Borderline Personality Disorders for Dummies by Charles H. Elliot and Laura L. Smith.

Girl, Interrupted (synopsis) by Mark Deming

Girl, Interrupted (movie review) by Peter Stack

The Catcher in the Rye by J.D. Salinger

"What's in a Name? -- The Outlook for Borderline Personality Disorder," National Institute for Mental Health, April, 2010; March 2, 2011; by Insel, Thomas.

"Holden Caulfield -- BPD symptoms" by Sean Reddish (online).

Lethal Intent by Sue Russell

The Borderline Personality Disorder Survival Guide by Alexander Chapman and Kim Gratz

Memory, Pain and the Truth by Maura Dolan, Los Angeles Times, June 21, 2005.

Witness for the Defense by Elizabeth Loftus and Katherine Ketcham

Distortions in the Memory of Children by Elizabeth Loftus and J.M. Doyle, *Journal of Social Issues*, 1984

Four Films of Woody Allen by Woody Allen & Marshall Brickman

The Seinfeld Scripts by Larry David & Jerry Seinfeld

Diagnostic Statistical Manual of Mental Disorders, APA, 2000.

Psychodynamic Psychotherapy of Borderline Patients by O.F. Kernberg, M.A. Selzer

The Interpersonal Theory of Psychiatry by H.S. Sullivan

Treatment of Borderline Personality Disorder with *Psychoanalytically Oriented Partial Hospitalization* by A. Bateman in *American Journal of Psychiatry* 2001

Cognitive Therapy of Personality Disorders by A.T. Beck

Dialectical Behavior Therapy for Borderline Personality Disorder by M.M. Linehan, *Bulletin of the Menninger Clinic*, 1987

Treating Personality Fragmentation and Dissociation in *Borderline Personality Disorder: A Pilot Study of the Impact of Cognitive Analytic Therapy* by A. Wildgoose, *British Journal of Medical Psychology*, 2001

Relapse Prevention by G.A. Marlett, 1985

The Theory and Practice of Group Psychotherapy by I.D. Yalom, 1985

Biological and Pharmacological Aspects of Borderline Personality Disorder by E.F. Coccaro, *Hospital and Community Psychiatry*, 1991.

Is There Any Drug Treatment of Choice for the Borderline Patient? By P.H. Soloff, *Acta Psychiatric Scandinavia*, 1994.

Alcoholics Anonymous (basic book), Alcoholics Anonymous World Services, Inc.

The Al-Anon Family Groups -- Classic Edition

Borderline Personality Disorder Demystified by Robert E. Friedel, 2004.

American Psychiatric Association: Practice Guideline for the Treatment of Patients with Borderline Personality Disorder. Am J Psychiatry, 2001.

Printed in Great Britain
by Amazon.co.uk, Ltd.,
Marston Gate.